Going To Law School

Preparing for a
Transformative Experience

*Timely advice and insight
from an award-winning
lawyer, law professor,
and law school dean*

Nelson P. Miller

Going to law school: preparing for a transformative experience.

Miller, Nelson P.

Published by:

Crown Management LLC – October 2016

1527 Pineridge Drive
Grand Haven, MI 49417
USA

ISBN: 978-0-9980601-1-8

Contents

I. Why Law School?

A. Opportunity

Law school presents you with a fabulous and fascinating educational opportunity leading to the most meaningful of service careers. Far from involving simply memorizing many laws and rules, law school instead challenges you to articulate the legitimate goals of persons and institutions in every imaginable social setting, while discerning how best to guide, promote, or constrain actions meant to achieve those goals. Lawyers must recognize their clients' interests and commitments, and then interpret and advance those interests and commitments within the rich context of differing interests and commitments of other persons and institutions. How do we all get along, and not just get along, but flourish? Lawyers don't have their own dreams as much as help others achieve their dreams, which is a service mission that makes for its own richly satisfying dream. Law school helps you learn means, methods, skills, and processes to accomplish an enormously useful and personally satisfying professional service mission.

B. Challenge

To help you accomplish that educational goal of equipping yourself for hugely satisfying professional service, though, law school must present you with substantial intellectual challenges. Societies have learned over the course of millennia that law subjects, constructs, structures, and principles must be many, comprehensive, subtle, and detailed, and yet also resonant, powerful, organized, and thematic, in order for law and lawyers to work effectively in administering a flourishing society of rich

1

liberty and opportunity. Lawyers have no magic lever or wand. Your skill as a lawyer is not to incant the same magic words over many different circumstances and situations. Rather, you must know the source, structure, goals, and processes of law to deploy law in effective service of your clients. Clients don't hire stupid lawyers. They retain lawyers whose wisdom, skill, and insight can shape their futures for the better. Law school can only equip you with these special skills and foster in you these special attributes by challenging you intellectually to a degree that no other program has yet challenged you.

C. Reasons

Given the magnitude of both your opportunity and your challenge, the first key then for preparing for and succeeding in law school is to confirm why you are pursuing a law degree. Law students bring to law school all kinds of goals and ambitions. Nearly all of those ambitions are highly laudatory and worthwhile. Most students are correct in believing that law school can help them achieve their specific individual goals. Importantly, law school's role is not to change student ambitions but instead to fulfill and amplify them. Yet students do not always have a clear view of their goals or how law school can help students reach them. Another role of law school in addition to helping students achieve their career goals is to help students explore and expand those goals and ambitions. Yes, reflect on why you are pursuing a law degree. Preserve your goals and ambitions by writing them down now. But at the same time, don't be too concerned if you are unclear in your specific goals. Instead, begin now to explore, examine, and clarify those goals. Consider the following examples of students who had varying goals entering law school and discovered gradually how law school helped to clarify, fulfill, and in some instances modify those goals. Let these examples help you reflect on and write your own law school and law career goals.

2

D. Reinvention

John went to law school to reinvent himself. John had been a successful producer of small films, working with creative directors, actors, and other artists, while making his way in a fascinating, fluid, and competitive business environment. Yet as much as he could see that he was succeeding within that industry, and as much as he enjoyed the work and relationships, he also felt like he was not yet whom, or what, he should be. Always an avid reader, John discerned from the breadth and depth of his reading that he somehow needed to make himself anew, if not exactly to start over, then to in some way *reinvent* his career. Although married and responsible for his growing family's support, John worked out a plan with his wife that he would dive into law school, do his very best academically while being prudent financially, and see where his new knowledge and skills would take him.

Not long later, after working hard and effectively through law school, John had become a well-respected and highly valued associate at a large law firm with multiple offices. John found himself putting together film-production and other business deals both for the firm's clients and clients whom he brought to the firm from his prior artistic work. Always an early adopter of technology, John was also leading the firm in its exploration and adoption of social-media platforms for client support and marketing. True to his commitments, and while every bit a full-time employee of his law firm, John was also helping on the side to lead a music-recording ministry for youth while also helping to organize and manage other ministries around the city and state. The new knowledge and skills that law school had helped John acquire had given him new service opportunities and influence, while his burgeoning career in law practice with a major firm had given John a steady financial and resource base. John had reinvented himself through law school. Given his passion about personal growth, John also now helps other professionals tell their own stories of reinvention.

E. Extension

Marina went to law school to extend her already-rich ministry to the poor. Marina's parents had been missionaries in Singapore, and so Marina had long known what a heart-led, passionate life looked like in commitment to the service of others. Indeed, even before starting law school, Marina had worked for a local nonprofit and intentionally lived among the urban poor for whom she would found her own nonprofit right after law school. Marina wasn't sure that law school would enable her to retain those commitments. She had some concern that law school would alter or at least challenge her core commitments. Although she wasn't certain that law school was just the right next step, Marina did know that the one thing that she wanted out of law school was to extend her ministry to poor urban youth. She wanted to have greater impact in areas and communities in which she already had some influence. She wanted to do more. And so drawing on her contacts developed as a law student, Marina organized child-law events and conferences, brought a state supreme court justice into the law school to speak about child-law reform, and won grants with which to employ other law students to research and write on law reform.

Marina found in law school that she had an extraordinary capacity for learning law, graduating first in her law school class, Marina then worked as a research attorney for her state's mid-level appellate court. Her sterling academic record, outstanding writing skill, and successful judicial internships had earned Marina prompt and stable placement with the appellate court. Yet even though her new job gave her high reputation with solid income and great job security and benefits, Marina quickly realized that she hadn't gone to law school for that job. She had instead gone to law school to extend her urban ministry. So after just seven months, Marina left her new job in favor of solo practice in her own new small firm. Before she started law school, Marina had the impression that the last thing she would ever do was to defend clients facing criminal charges. Now, though, she realized that doing so would give her the greatest positive influence over the most desperately challenged and poor. Within a few short years, Marina was among the leading defense lawyers in her locale. She was also teaching prisoners legal research and writing, teaching law-related courses to undergraduates, and continuing to lead her nonprofit. Marina had indeed extended her ministry and influence far beyond that which she had even hoped.

F. Affinity

Julia went to law school to study business law to further promote the self-sufficiency and welfare of her Native-American tribe. Julia had many of the same desires and commitments that her classmates had to improve their own lives morally, financially, materially, and socially. Yet she also had a special affinity for her tribe. While she had not grown up on the reservation, her close Native friends and her father celebrated their Native-American culture and tradition. Julia knew from these experiences that her tribe and others like it had substantial financial and social needs and opportunities, many of them requiring sophisticated professional support. She could also see that the tribes were not always getting that professional support, at least not always from professionals who shared in the respect for and commitment to the culture and welfare of Native-American tribes. Law school gave Julia an opportunity to pursue both her own personal goals and the goals and interests of Native-American tribes with whom she held an affinity. She learned in law school the knowledge, skills, and ethics that other students learned, but she also focused her studies on constitutional law, commercial law, and other areas where she felt that she would develop the knowledge and skills to promote tribal interests, especially those related to business and economic development. Along the way, she met mentors who helped her discern the knowledge and skills that she would need. Best of all, she completed an internship and clerkship with her Tribe and an externship with a specialized business court.

Right after graduation and passing the bar exam, Julia began work as an associate attorney at a small majority Native-owned national firm that only represents Native-American tribes and their wholly owned businesses. She knew that tribal law can be complex. Tribal sovereignty affects the application of state and federal law. The laws, rules, and procedures under which tribal businesses operate can be quite different from the state and federal law applicable to other businesses that she had studied in law school. Yet Julia found immediate satisfaction in parsing those complexities in order to be able to advise tribes and their businesses on clear ways forward. She could see the impact of her law services on the success of the tribal businesses, the revenue from which directly benefit the social and economic welfare of the tribes and their individual members. She had suspected that law practice would be impactful, meaningful, and satisfying. Julia's only surprise was just how immediate and profound the impact of her law services could be. Of course, some days were harder than others, but yet hardly a day went by without her thinking of and drawing on her own tribal affinity while appreciating the opportunity to serve her tribal clients. She certainly had plenty of that impactful work, too. Julia even had the opportunity of working with her law school to hire a new law clerk as the firm considered further expansion. Julia had fulfilled her affinity.

G. Fulfillment

Mark went to law school to fulfill his life's mission to improve conditions for disabled adults and children. Mark's interest in the rights of the young and disabled stemmed from his own congenital condition that had kept him to a wheelchair throughout his life. He had written policy papers in his undergraduate program in public administration and looked forward to law school, thinking that it might well be more of the same policy advocacy that he found so personally fulfilling. Initially, though, law school hadn't seemed to be a good fit for Mark who struggled with the precise analysis of claims, causes, and charges that law school's first-year curriculum required. Rather than mope or quit when the school required him to take time off before restarting, Mark launched himself back into college coursework in his disability-rights field, this time paying particular attention to thoughtful analysis. He then flew through law school, finding his third-year clinical work representing family members in divorce and custody disputes enormously energizing and satisfying. Best of all, though, during law school Mark met and married his wife, a nursing student with similar disability who, like Mark, was becoming both a skilled advocate and clinician preparing to serve the most vulnerable.

Not long later, Mark was in a busy solo law practice in a rural part of the south to which he and his wife had moved for his wife's job and graduate studies. Mark initially represented mostly indigent defendants in court appointments but gradually expanded his practice to include serving all of the several legal needs of the poorer residents of his community, among whom his reputation for committed and caring advocacy grew. On his best days, Mark could see how his clients were slowly improving their lives both in drawing on his professional skills but also in imitating his own overcomer's attitude. On his hardest days, Mark could still see in his clients their perseverance and hope that he, better than anyone else in his community, knew would see them through. Fulfillment didn't come wrapped up as a nice little gift, Mark knew. He had instead earned the respect of his wife, community, family, and self through an unwavering commitment to others. Mark could look back with great satisfaction on where he had started and how far he had come, knowing that he had much yet to achieve. In his growing law practice, he felt that he was once again laying the groundwork of experience and refining the skill that would make him an even greater advocate for the young, disadvantaged, and disabled people about whom he so deeply cared.

H. Exploration

Steven went to law school to learn what chapter was next. As a college junior pre-med and math major at a select university, Steven had won appointment to NASA's Space Command Program, meaning that he was on his way to achieving his long-planned life goal of being an astronaut. Then the Challenge space shuttle exploded, killing several highly skilled astronauts, putting manned flights on hold, and ending Steven's opportunity. From that point on, Steven stopped planning and started exploring. He became a lieutenant in the Air Force reserve, developed a financial-education website, worked for a multinational computer maker, owned a prominent restaurant and marina, sold investments, and became a bank vice president. Then he went to law school, sensing that doing so would increase his knowledge and strategic skill for executive-level management. Drawing on his military discipline and life skills, Steven excelled in law school. While finishing his law degree, he took the time to serve as a research and drafting clerk at two large law firms that provided services to the kinds of corporate clients for whom he had once worked as a manager or executive. He was, in other words, outstandingly qualified for the work. Both firms offered him a position right out of law school.

Today, Steven remains an attorney at the large corporate-services firm that hired him at graduation. His knowledge of his corporate clients' needs and concerns, plus his financial skills, make Steven a very effective lawyer for clients. His knowledge of how organizations work and his character both for leadership and teamwork make Steven a very effective employee of his law firm. Law school turned out to be the perfect challenge and opportunity for him at just the right time, expanding and improving his already well-developed skills. Law practice with a major firm also turned out to be just the right career move at just the right time, giving Steven broader-than-ever experience serving a diverse corporate clientele using his varied expert skills. Steven will continue to explore. His next step could be developing new business and practice areas for the firm, management at the firm, supporting new ventures for his clients, or something completely unpredictable, as Steven long ago learned. The key, Steven knows, is to keep exploring while walking through the open door.

Study. Read, reflect, and investigate until you can name three lawyers whom you admire and be able to explain to a friend or family member why you admire them. The lawyers whom you choose may be historical figures like Cicero, Lincoln, Thurgood Marshall, or Sandra Day O'Connor, or current well-known government lawyers like Preet Bharara, Eric Holder, or Loretta Lynch, or family members, neighbors, acquaintances, or friends.

II. What Is Law School?

To make the most of law school, you should first appreciate what law school is. To the nation, law schools are the institutions that educate the professionals who ensure a society that is at once orderly, secure, prosperous, and lasting, and yet in which individuals have the greatest liberty to pursue and benefit from their own ends. Make no mistake: lawyers are economic drivers, creating, preserving, and promoting the liberty, property, and other conditions under which individuals and their families, firms, foundations, and other organizations strive most fairly in order to flourish. The first thing that a leader would do to destroy society and impose anarchy, as Shakespeare so eloquently asserted, would be to kill all the lawyers. Conversely, the first thing that a leader would do to create the conditions for prosperity would be to establish the rule of law, that which is only possible with a skilled profession dedicated to doing so. Law is also the sister study to theology. Lawyers are ministers of God's own justice, that which, while just, is also equitable, egalitarian, restorative, and redemptive. You may not be going to law school for any of these grandly selfless reasons. Yet even if not, then still appreciate the place that your own personal ambitions, laudable as they doubtless are, have within their larger social, philosophical, spiritual, and historical contexts.

A. Missions

Within that larger context, law schools have varying educational missions. Those variations can significantly affect the curriculum and programs of the particular school. For instance, some law schools see their role as preparing graduates to join large firms that serve national and multinational corporate

11

interests. Those schools may draw their professors from among graduates of Ivy League law schools who served clerkships with the federal courts that hear and decide diversity-jurisdiction disputes protecting those national and multinational corporations against local interests. Other law schools pursue a clinical and practical mission to prepare graduates to serve a broader and more diverse array of individual and local interests. Still other law schools emphasize scholarship and policy development drawing on environmental, social-justice, feminist, race-theory, and other critiques and other inter-disciplinary studies. Some law schools have faith-centered missions or missions connected with other social or historical movements. Law school websites declare their schools' mission with varying degrees of specificity and clarity. Examine the school's stated mission, but also examine faculty biographies and program focuses to see what the school and those who operate it actually do and value.

B. Standards

While law schools vary in their missions and those variations can be significant, accredited law schools must still meet relatively specific standards that make law schools alike in many other respects. The U.S. Department of Education authorizes the American Bar Association's Council on Legal Education and Admission to the Bar to accredit law schools. The ABA publishes standards that law schools must meet to maintain their accreditation. Those standards require a law school to instruct students in the knowledge, skills, and ethics that competent lawyers require to obtain and maintain their licensure. ABA standards further require law schools to provide skills instruction including writing instruction and instruction in clinical practice, unless the student already has experience doing legal work under a lawyer. The next section summarizes the knowledge that law schools must generally impart for graduates to pass the bar and enter law practice. As to skills, the ABA's well-known MacCrate Report on law schools lists problem solving, law analysis and reasoning, law research, fact investigation, communication, client counseling, negotiation, litigation, practice management, and recognizing and resolving ethics issues. Another chapter below describes these skills in more detail, while yet another chapter addresses lawyer ethics.

C. Core Subjects

To obtain a law license, most lawyers must pass a state bar examination that includes as one component the multiple-choice format Multistate Bar Examination. Although law schools can vary widely in the elective courses and course subjects that they offer, the Multistate Bar Examination requirement for licensure creates consistency in the core subjects in which law schools instruct. The Multistate Bar Examination tests seven subjects: tort law, contract law, criminal law and procedure, constitutional law, civil procedure, property law, and evidence. Tort law studies liability for personal injury and property damage, the law of care, intrinsic worth, categorical imperative, or Golden Rule holding that we must act reasonably as to the interests of others. Contract law studies the making and enforcement of promises or covenants on which reliable transactions of all kinds, including personal and commercial transactions, depend. Criminal law studies the punishment and rehabilitation through which society sets bounds addressing the worst of human behavior. Constitutional law studies the founding document and associated principles through which the people have agreed to govern themselves. Civil procedure studies private dispute resolution through the courts and alternative forums. Property law studies the right to hold, convey, control, and benefit from lands and things. Evidence studies the rules by which we accept information as reliable in resolving criminal and civil disputes in the courts. Together, these seven subjects form law school's core curriculum. Many schools require courses in all seven subjects, while many other schools do not. Students graduating from a school that does not teach one or more of these subjects and yet planning on obtaining a law license must rely on a commercial bar-preparation course or other studies to master untaught subjects.

D. Other Common Subjects

Law schools commonly teach much more than the above seven core Multistate Bar Examination-tested subjects plus the skills, clinical practice, and ethics instruction that ABA standards require. Notice, for instance, that the above subject list does not include estate planning, family law, the law of business organizations, taxation, secured transactions (liens, mortgages, and other security interests used to secure financed transactions), worker's compensation law, energy law, or administrative law. All or any of these subjects, and dozens of other law subjects, could prove enormously useful to you in law practice, depending on the field or fields of law that you choose. Many state bar exams use essay questions beyond the multiple-choice Multistate Bar Examination to test these or other extra subjects. Don't worry, though. Each state bar publishes well in advance its list of tested subjects. As soon as you decide in which state you plan to license, you can find out exactly what extra subjects, if any, to study in law school to prepare for the bar exam. Yet law schools offer many more elective courses that have little or nothing to do with what a bar exam may test. Those elective courses include sports law, entertainment law, gun-control law, election law, nonprofit law, natural-resources law, art law, sustainability law, animal law, the law of agriculture, and dozens of others. You can and should fit the elective part of your law school's curriculum to your interests and planned career. Your faculty and career advisors in law school will help you do so.

E. Clinical Experiences

As the above section on accreditation standards suggests, law school does not end with classroom instruction in doctrinal subjects. Indeed, many law students and graduates feel that their education did not begin in earnest until they began their clinical experience. Lawyers once learned their profession not through law schools but through apprenticeships with practicing lawyers. A recent ground-breaking study of law schools titled *Educating Lawyers*, also known as the Carnegie Report, recognized that even today, effective law schools provide their students with forms of apprenticeship in all three law school dimensions of knowledge, skills, and ethics. Law schools have two primary ways in which they help students gain the required clinical experience. One way is through a clinic, often located in the law school but sometimes off site, in which a faculty member supervises students in the actual representation of real clients. A second way is through externships in which the school places a student with a practicing lawyer to do law work under that lawyer's supervision and the simultaneous supervision of a faculty member. One advantage of a clinic is that it runs like a law firm but one staffed largely by law students, giving students hands-on experience not only in representing clients but in case and file management, much like small-firm or solo practice. One advantage of an externship is that it immerses the student at a firm, agency, or other site where the student might have earned a job when the externship ends or the student graduates. In either case, students routinely rate their clinical experience as the most-significant and most-satisfying of their law school experience. Law practice is great—the sooner you can get to it, the better.

F. More Than the Sum

Yet law school is more than the sum of these many parts along its knowledge, skills, and ethics dimensions. Yes, law school's core subjects are profound, teaching you how society orders and maintains itself. Law school's elective subjects are fascinating, attractive, and diverse, capturing your passions and preparing you to serve such varied persons, populations, communities, causes, and interests. Law school's skills courses equip you for such effective problem solving, solution generating, and creative and caring intellectual and affective work. Law school's professional-responsibility courses help you see why and how masterful lawyers serve. And law school's clinical experiences help you take the last step of integrating law knowledge with professional skills and lawyer ethics. But law school is still something larger than this sum of its parts. Law school changes you for the better. It helps you see the world both as it truly is,

15

rather than as too many of us poorly imagine it, but also as it truly should be, in the way that many more of us wish. Law school is practical and profound, capable of preserving the best of your commitments while equipping you with more-specific vision, stronger character, and special skills. Like other professional programs, law school is largely what you make of it. Yet unlike some other professional programs, law school can help to transform you by connecting you with a career that promotes human flourishing.

Study. Rank the following opportunities of law school in the order that you most value them: (a) learning sound doctrine; (b) becoming more logical; (c) acquiring communication skills; (d) becoming a better writer; (e) maturing in your ethics; (f) exploring new fields; (g) discerning a service career; (h) connecting with new communities; and (i) personal transformation.

III. Is Law School Worth It?

To make the most of law school, you should also recognize both its cost and value, in other words, understand and appreciate the economics of a law career. If you do not believe that law school is a good investment of your time and tuition, then you may not pursue the education with the confidence and commitment that your investment deserves. Conversely, if you believe that law school is a good investment but cannot articulate why, then you may later find others unnecessarily shaking your confidence in your investment and by doing so affecting your commitment and your investment's value to you. The students who gain the most from law school tend to be those who know best both its cost and value, and prepare themselves to navigate both cost and value most effectively. Law school is in that respect like other investments requiring both your time and treasure: you largely get out of it what you put into it. The ceiling is high. You could end up quite successful financially and in other ways. Yet the floor is also low. If you don't put the education and your school's programs and resources to good effect, then you could end up owing substantial educational debt, not find the employment for which you hoped, and not find financial and other success. The good news is that the medians and averages, meaning what happens to and for most law graduates and lawyers, are still healthy, as they have been for a long time. Most students who attend law school, graduate, and pursue a career find acceptable success. Consider the following data, principles, and strategies to be sure that you do as well as you hoped and as well as you and your investment deserve.

A. Tuition

Learn the financial cost of law school. Law schools help you with that effort by publishing cost estimates on their websites. Law school programs vary widely in their cost. To begin, tuition rates vary widely. Be sure to compare and contrast tuition rates, especially net tuition rates after the school applies any scholarships. Law school tuition data is widely available, even on single cost-comparison websites. Some law schools will also help you calculate your probable scholarship, even before you apply. Seek scholarships from the law school and from other sources such as professional organizations, affinity organizations, volunteer associations, charitable organizations, foundations, and denominations or other faith organizations. Many law students substantially reduce their tuition through school and other-source scholarships. Use tuition and scholarship information to determine your *net* tuition, which is the first cost figure that truly matters. The number, value, and terms of the scholarships that law schools and other sources offer also vary widely. Be sure that you understand the terms, particularly whether you will retain beyond the first term or first year the scholarship that the school or other source initially offers you. Some schools and sources let you keep a scholarship as long as you remain in good standing, while other schools and sources require that you maintain a high grade-point average (higher than all students receiving scholarships will be able to muster). Don't count on a scholarship to last throughout law school unless the terms warrant it.

B. Other Costs

The cost of law school, though, is not all about base tuition or even net after-scholarship tuition rates. The cost of living near enough to the school to attend also varies widely. Manhattan and downtown Chicago are more-expensive law school locales than many others. What you save in tuition you may spend in rental housing, transportation, parking, food, child care, and other living costs. Develop a budget to compare and contrast costs. Project what you will spend at each location. Plan to reduce living costs.

18

Track your spending now, and reduce where you are able. What you save now, you can consume and enjoy later. Also, consider what you will earn or not earn while in law school. The biggest cost of law school can be forgone income, particularly if you are not working while in law school. If you are able to attend law school part time while continuing your current employment, then you may be significantly reducing your forgone income and saving significant hidden law-school costs. Alternatively, if you are able to assume new employment while in law school, preferably but not necessarily related to your law studies, then you also be able to significantly reduce your forgone income and save hidden educational costs. Consider federal work-study employment with your law school. Working while in law school may require that you take fewer courses and thus spread your education over a longer time but could still make good economic sense, depending on your earned income. Schools that offer evening, weekend, and summer programs can facilitate work schedules. Another option that a special law school program may offer is to accelerate the traditional three-year program into two years so that you graduate into higher-income law work sooner with less forgone income.

C. Employment

Cost is only one side of the financial ledger, though. The other side is the earnings that you should expect a law degree to enable or facilitate. First consider broad and reliable data on lawyer employment. U.S. Bureau of Labor Statistics show that at the last recession's beginning in 2008, America numbered 1,034,000 lawyers, among whom 1,014,000 were employed and 20,000 were unemployed for a 1.9% pre-recession unemployment rate among lawyers. The Bureau reports that at the end of 2015, America lawyers numbered 1,173,000, among whom 1,160,000 were employed and 13,000 were unemployed, for just a 1.1% lawyer unemployment rate. In other words, in the seven years following the recession's onset, the nation added 139,000 lawyers, the number of employed lawyers grew by 146,000, and the number of unemployed lawyers fell by 7,000. In 2014 and 2015 combined,

19

the nation added 60,000 lawyers, saw an increase of 68,000 employed lawyers, and experienced a decrease of 8,000 unemployed lawyers. The public confuses lawyer unemployment, which is plainly quite low, with unemployment of recent law school graduates. The National Association for Law Placement reports just under 10% unemployment among recent graduates seeking employment. Recent graduates are not lawyers until admitted to practice. Because 15% to 20% of law graduates nationally do not pass the bar exam on the first try, they may not gain employment as lawyers for some time after graduation. Eventually, most graduates become lawyers, as the above favorable employment numbers and unemployment percentages demonstrate. Given fewer law school graduates and increasing lawyer retirements, the good national lawyer-employment picture may continue to improve.

D. Earnings

Lawyers on the whole make a decent living. According to the U.S. Bureau of Labor Statistics, the annual average wage of lawyers was $131,990 in 2013, $133,470 in 2014, and $136,260 in 2015, consistent with increases every year since 1997 when the Bureau first made these figures readily available. Average figures are higher than medians (half of all lawyers above and half below the median figure). The Bureau of Labor Statistics reports 2014 median lawyer income at $114,970. Lawyer income varies widely. The Bureau reports the 2014 75th percentile lawyer income at $172,540 versus the 25th percentile lawyer income at $75,630, while of course some lawyers make more than the 75th percentile (in a few cases much more) while an equal number make less than the 25th percentile. Lawyer earnings also vary from field to field and geographic area to geographic area, with lawyers in San Jose, California earning a $201,240 average annual salary but lawyers in rural areas earning a fraction of 2014's $133,470 national annual average. Bureau statistics show that at 2014 average annual income of $133,470, lawyers earn substantially more than do others in nearly all other social-service jobs such as patrol officers ($59,560), high school teachers ($59,330), and paralegals ($51,840).

Most significantly for new lawyers, starting income is lower than income for experienced lawyers, as is true in many other fields and professions. Overall, though, a widely cited 2013 study by finance/economics and law professors McIntyre and Simkovic associated a law degree with 73% median earnings increases, 60% hourly wage increases, and $57,200 annual average earnings increases, equating to an approximate $1 million pretax lifetime earnings value, against which to measure the above costs.

E. Financing Law School

How you pay for your law education can significantly affect its cost to you and the opportunities that it creates for you. The ideal would be to pay for the education out of savings and current earnings so as to avoid the interest and opportunity costs that borrowing entails. Just as is true for a home mortgage or other substantial indebtedness, interest can compound educational debt into a multiple of the borrowed principal. Keeping borrowing to a minimum is therefore wise. Yet except for the few students who receive very substantial scholarships, few other students are able to pay without borrowing, often substantial borrowing particularly when they have already financed their undergraduate education. Educational debt exceeding $150,000 is not unusual, with some students borrowing over $200,000. Students eligible for federal loans can fund the cost of their education, but don't borrow just because the money is available. Be very cautious in accumulating debt of this or any similar magnitude. Work to reduce or eliminate the balance on credit cards, vehicle, and other loans before starting law school. Avoid incurring new debt such as for a vehicle while incurring debt for education. When ready to borrow, complete your federal loan application forms at the U.S. Department of Education website www.studentloans.gov. Law students qualifying for federal loans may borrow up to the cost of their graduate education first through the Federal Unsubsidized Loan program and then the Graduate PLUS Loan program. To access these programs, you will need to complete the Free Application for Federal Student Aid (FAFSA) form, Entrance Counseling form, Master Promissory Note for Federal

21

Unsubsidized Loan, Master Promissory Note for Graduate PLUS Loan, Graduate PLUS Loan Application, and Credit Check Application. Expect to begin the loan-application process around three months before beginning law school. Meet with law school financial-aid personnel to review your budget and ensure that you are borrowing wisely.

Study. Do you know where you stand with your personal finances? Do you have a personal balance sheet (written record of assets and liabilities)? What are your financial goals? Can you list three important financial principles? If you wish to explore sound financial goals and principles, then read *Lawyer Finances: Principles and Practices for Personal and Professional Financial Success.*

IV. Which Law School?

A. Choices

So now you have sound ideas of why you are pursuing law school. In which law school, though, should you enroll? Most law students have choices of which law school to attend. Make the best choice. Your choice of schools can affect your law school success. Some law schools are better places for certain students to learn than are other law schools. Academic-support programs and personnel (both faculty and staff) differ from school to school. Schedules, tuition and other costs, scholarships, and other variables from school to school can also influence how effectively you learn and how supportive the school will be of your educational goals. Some faculties are more dedicated to scholarship than to practice, service, or teaching. Some programs are more practical and clinical while others are more theoretical and academic. Some staff members are better trained at and more committed to student service. Some schools have only traditional programs and schedules while others have multiple program and schedule options. Student bodies also differ, some relatively more uniform in income, ideology, worldview, values, and other demographics while others less so. Some schools will be far from home while others closer. The communities in which law schools locate are also different, some metropolitan while others suburban, some public college or university while others private and professional. Visit the law schools that seem to make the most sense for you. Interview the dean, faculty members, staff, and students. Choose your best fit, and you are likely to do better in law school.

23

B. Culture

The prior section intimates that while location, programs, schedules, cost, and other objective criteria can all be important to your choice of the right law school for you, the school's or its particular campus's culture could prove equally or more important to you in helping you achieve your educational goals. Groups naturally develop and communicate to their members varying social norms, customs, conventions, attitudes, behaviors, and approaches. Law school campuses are no different in that respect. One law school's campus culture may communicate highly positive norms of engagement, collaboration, accessibility, affinity, respect, and support. Another law school's campus culture may be less collaborative while more competitive, and less challenging and engaging while more lenient or relaxed. Some campus cultures promote social and ideological conformity while others are more inclusive, tolerant, and diverse. Some are welcoming, others formal. Some recognize and celebrate primarily traditional forms of academic achievement like high grade-point averages and class standing, while others more-often recognize and celebrate non-traditional forms of academic achievement like service activities and student leadership. You may find it hard to discern a particular campus's culture, but current students can often describe that culture quite clearly, giving prominent examples, too. When you have narrowed your school choice, make an effort to visit the campus not just to meet with administrators, faculty, and staff but also to meet and chat with current students.

C. Rankings

Avoid the rankings game. Rankings are both gamed and misleading. Law schools know that students give far too much weight to rankings. Students think that to get a job they must go to the highest-ranked school into which they can get, when to the contrary study has shown that only the very top students at the very top-of-the-rankings schools get jobs based on their law school. What you *learn* in law school is what matters, not where

24

you *go* to law school. Students also think that the top-ranked schools have better professors and instruction. To the contrary, law professors improve their school's ranking by publishing, not teaching. Instructional quality, including your accessibility to your professors and their knowledge of sound instructional practices and your particular needs, may be much better at lower-ranked schools where faculty members put you before publishing. Law schools also know how to skew the rankings by denying you admission through the front door in the first year but then taking large numbers of you through the back door on transfer in the second year so that they can report higher entering first-year LSAT scores. Law schools engage in these deceptive practices despite knowing that the practices adversely affect minority students in particular. Don't be a victim of the rankings game. Every law school has its advantages and disadvantages. Choose based on those factors, not rankings.

D. Profiles

Don't try to attend a law school where everyone else is like you. You won't find any such law school. You and every other student are unique. Even if you could find such a law school where every other student was just like you, then it wouldn't be a good place for you to encounter students with the differing experiences, interests, ambitions, needs, and perspectives that would help you learn what others discern and how they behave differently than you. My law school, for instance, has young academic superstars who could go to other law schools but attend my campus for its unique location, varied schedule options, strong learning culture, and accessible faculty with strong service commitments and tons of practical experience. Yet my law school also has older students seeking a second or third career, working students seeking to advance in their current career, family breadwinners (often single parents) seeking to increase their financial security, and passionate advocates seeking to gain greater influence over their cause. When I ask new students why they chose to go to law school and then chose my campus and school, each new student reflects a unique combination of needs,

25

interests, and ambitions. I encourage new students to examine, record, and speak about those needs, interests, and ambitions, and not just with family members and law school faculty and staff but also with new classmates. Finding your own deliberate, well-thought-out path into and through law school involves articulating and rearticulating that path to yourself and others while hearing the same from others. You have choices. Make them wisely for your own sound reasons, and you will do better.

E. Goals

Know and achieve your own goals, not someone else's. The herd is a powerful instinct. Despite that we have minds, wills, and choices, we tend so strongly simply to do as others do. Yet just because others are pursuing corporate work at a large firm after graduating from a very expensive law school, public-interest work at an advocacy organization after a highly academic legal education, or a federal judicial clerkship after enduring mind-numbing coursework at a prestigious law school, doesn't mean that you must do so, too. Corporate work at a large firm, public-interest work at an advocacy organization, or a federal judicial clerkship can all be exciting, satisfying, and rewarding goals to pursue. You can achieve those goals attending many different law schools. But they may not be your goals. Unless you know your goals, law school could induce you to assume goals that you would in retrospect rather not have pursued. If you don't know your goals but know that you want to attend law school, then choose a law school that will expose you to many different career options and help you investigate and explore each. Ask to speak with both recent and senior alumni of the law schools that you are visiting to see how their school helped them choose and attain a satisfying career.

Study. In five minutes or less, write your law-school and law-career goals. Then take a few more minutes to revise your goals after reflecting on the following questions. How confident are you that what you first recorded are indeed your goals? How achievable are your goals? What public and private purposes do your goals serve? Whom do your goals serve? How do your goals connect with your commitments, passions, and beliefs?

V. Who Will Help?

A. Supporters

While law schools vary in their degree and variety of academic support, expect to have help in law school. Many law students are self-starters. Law students tend to be organized, prefer organization from others, be task oriented, and persist in sound practices and disciplines. You need not and should not treat law school, though, as a solo venture. You will learn more, learn more quickly, and acquire important additional interpersonal, communication, and network skills when you work closely with at least a few others in law school. Your professors are obviously your primary help in learning law knowledge, skills, and ethics. You need not learn from your professor solely in the classroom or through exercises and materials that your professor posts for you online. Your professor will also be available to you outside of class, whether to answer your questions, review your written work, or provide guidance on study habits and resources. Your professor may also be willing to retain you as a teaching or research assistant, from which you can also learn. Fellow students are others with whom and from whom you will also learn. The vast majority of law students gain at least some benefit in at least some courses some of the time from having study partners, participating in study groups, offering or receiving peer tutoring, and engaging in other peer-to-peer learning. Staff members at the law school are also your learning resource including not only those designated and trained for academic support but also career counselors, program directors, and librarians. Deans and other school administrators can also provide you with substantial guidance. Make a point of regularly engaging these professionals on your behalf. Consider a few examples below.

B. Law Professors

Paul Sorensen practiced law at a major corporate-services law firm for nearly three decades before joining a law school faculty full time. His goal in doing so was simply to help train the next generation of skilled and ethical lawyers. After a long and very successful law career, Professor Sorensen felt that he had little left to accomplish in that career beyond ensuring that he gave richly back to the profession that had given him so much. He had already been the president of the local bar association, federal bar association, and courthouse-based law-help nonprofit provider, all volunteer roles that helped to ensure the integrity of the local state and federal courts, local lawyers, and access-to-justice programs. While he had thought some about becoming a judge, he just couldn't see another role beyond teaching law that would give him as much positive influence over the community and the law profession that was so critical to the community's welfare. So he began teaching law, first as a visiting professor and then before long as a full-time, tenured faculty member. Although he loved to teach upper-level students a negotiation-skills course with his lawyer wife and other prominent lawyers with whom he had worked over the years, Professor Sorensen's primary teaching subjects included first-year courses in tort law and contract law, and an upper-level required course in the law of remedies.

Not long after starting full time, Professor Sorensen had won the student vote as best professor of the term, competing against beloved law professors who had taught for and built their reputations over decades. While students liked many things about Professor Sorensen's instruction, students emphasized three things in their anonymous administrative evaluations of Professor Sorensen every term: (1) he and his materials were so clear about the law that no student could misunderstand or miss the important points; (2) he was so civil, kind, and professional that no student could mistake what the profession expected of a fine lawyer; and (3) he was so consistently accessible that students knew that he was teaching only for their benefit, not for his own scholarship, ego, finances, or reputation. He genuinely cared about each student and demonstrated that care in many different remarkable ways, some of them even anonymously. His one professed regret at the end of each term was that certain students hadn't come to see him in his office for help with the law subjects he was teaching or for career counseling or other support, advice, and guidance.

C. Students

Mary was pretty concerned about starting law school at her point in life. Her concerns were not about the academics. As a mature, skilled, and experienced professional in a publishing and marketing career, she knew that she could learn law and do well, indeed very well. Mary savored that intellectual opportunity and challenge. Yet her larger concern was how she would fit law school into her several other significant roles as the supportive wife of another successful and well-engaged full-time professional, a mother of talented teenage and pre-teen children, a career consultant on significant projects, and a valued community member. If law school was going to work on top of all of her other responsibilities, then Mary was going to need help. And indeed, she found that help, first from thoughtful, well-organized, accessible staff members who helped her arrange and order her courses and schedule, among other things to ensure most efficient use of her precious time. Then, her professors were equally organized and accommodating, ensuring that her studies were effective, efficient, and most of all productive. Administrators were helpful, too, whenever some matter came up that required insight, support, action, and advice.

Mary found her greatest support, though, from among her classmates. She made many new friends, of course, even inviting a large group of them to her home when at the end of a term it was time to relax and recharge. Among her classmates, she also

31

found a few study partners, one in particular with whom she shared notes, resources, and support when either of them was absent or felt the need for a little extra moral support. In her relationships with classmates, all of whom were also bright and mature, and whose varied educations, careers, and experiences made them especially diverse, Mary found that she was confirming and refining maturities in her own character. Indeed, odd though it seemed at the time, in retrospect it felt perfectly natural for her to have taken on a special role of caring and advocating for all of her classmates, somewhat as she cared and advocated for her own maturing children. She was not only drawing on the support of classmates for skills and insights that she had not yet perfected but was also drawing on her own considerable skills and insights to support her classmates in ways that they most needed and benefitted from her support. She hadn't initially thought that she was going to law school as much for her classmates as for herself, but she didn't regret in the least that she had the ability and willingness to take on that supporting role. In doing so, she also felt that she may have discovered something important about how she would use her law degree.

D. Staff Members

Danielle Hall practiced law with a small estate-planning firm before deciding to help her law school open a new campus by taking a full-time job as the campus's career counselor. While she had enjoyed practicing law, particularly the client service and interaction but also dealing daily with her practice area's technical aspects, Danielle found that she loved to promote professional growth and development even more. She had been president of the region's women lawyers association (a volunteer leadership position) for exactly that purpose, to help promote the careers and professional development of already-outstanding professionals whose ambitions were to do even better and even more. She found that she had a keen eye for professional character, personality, demeanor, and identity. Even as a lawyer and volunteer board president, Danielle had wanted new professionals to represent themselves well and to find engaging new careers and opportunities. Her role as a career counselor for her own law school gave her the perfect opportunity to pursue that passion for the professional development and personal advancement of others. She could travel to law firms, prosecutor and public-defender offices, other government agencies, and corporate-counsel offices, both locally and around the country, to make network connections and investigate and secure career opportunities for new and experienced lawyers, while meeting and speaking daily with students, graduates, and alumni of her own law school. She could also work daily with students on selecting courses, programs, and activities to improve their knowledge, skills, and resumes, and in reviewing their cover letters, resumes, writing samples, and portfolios to ensure that they represented themselves helpfully, positively, and accurately.

Danielle has seen many changes in her more than decade of career services. The employment market for lawyers continued to grow, even as it went through its usual up-and-down, down-and-up cycles. Some practice areas like taxation and intellectual property remained recruiting hotspots, while new hot fields arose like healthcare, insurance, and financial regulation. Law firms and agencies recruited lawyers in different ways, particularly toward online applications, electronic portfolios, videoconference interviews, and related technologies. Danielle kept ahead of these changes and improved her placement knowledge, skills, and practices, through her membership in the national lawyer-placement association, conference attendance, and other professional development. She worked with her campus dean to develop an orderly placement program for students and graduates to use. Yet through many changes, Danielle found her constant inspiration in the earnest ambition of individual students coming to her office one by one for advice and guidance. She also found much to show for her work including placement of graduates in large and small firms, at courts, agencies, and other government offices, and with corporate-counsel offices and other private employers of lawyers, all over the nation, indeed in locations around the world. Hardly a day went by when she didn't have some encouraging contact with or news of a student gaining a great new opportunity or graduate achieving a great new success.

E. Administrators

Tracey Brame had a varied, exciting, and satisfying law career before deciding to teach and administer at a law school as her next chapter as a professional. In law school, she interned with a nonprofit challenging death-penalty sentences, where she also helped prepare a Supreme Court argument and drafted racial-justice legislation. Her first stop after law school was the prestigious role of clerking for a federal judge in a major metropolitan area, although her judge and mentor didn't want her considerable talents limited to research alone and so had her also work for the federal defender's office and correctional facility. Dean Brame's next post was as an appellate advocate with the state appellate defender office, followed by a similar role with a federal defender office. Her next stop was the nation's capital Washington, D.C., where she served as a staff attorney for the district's public defender office. Marriage to another lawyer (a law school classmate) brought her to the city where she soon started at the law school after first working as a staff attorney at the city's legal aid office. Dean Brame's legal-aid work gave her an opportunity to develop her civil-justice rather than criminal-justice knowledge and skills, representing low-income and indigent clients in family law, housing, and consumer-law matters while also helping re-entering ex-offenders and using her Spanish-speaking skills.

Dean Brame first joined the law school as a full-time tenured professor to start her campus's clinic. Every accredited law school must offer its students clinical experiences. To satisfy that requirement, law schools maintain in-house clinics for students to practice law under a professor's supervision and external internships in which law students practice law under a supervising lawyer in a law firm or other professional setting. Dean Brame had soon established or helped to establish three clinics at her campus including a family-law clinic, municipal-law clinic, and public-defender clinic. She also taught courses on family law, racial justice, and the death penalty. Dean Brame's skill in advising and empathy in supporting students soon led the school to appoint her an assistant dean in addition even while she retained her professor and clinic-director duties. As an assistant dean, she works with students who faced special challenges such as illness or the death or illness of a close family member, to ensure that the student can complete academic work or withdraw temporarily in good standing. She also administers her campus's honor-code and discipline issues, in the event of any student misconduct. Law students must show their character and fitness to practice law. Dean Brame counsels and corrects students whose conduct threatens to skirt those requirements. She also works as a special-assistant U.S. attorney to involve law students in federal crime-prevention and community-relations programs. Her rich combination of teaching, service, and administrative roles have kept Dean Brame longer at the law school than in any of her several other lawyer careers. Those whose role is to support you in law school often find no more-rewarding career than doing so.

Study. Take just a minute to reflect on an educator, or if not an educator then a fellow student, who was especially helpful to you in your undergraduate program. Do you now expect to find similar help in law school? What habits or practices might you adopt in law school to ensure that you get adequate support while also helping other students locate and receive support?

VI. How Do I Prepare?

So now you have good ideas of why to attend law school and in which law school to enroll. Consider next a story illustrating why you might spend just a little time preparing for law school. A non-lawyer friend of mine who owned a trout farm taught me an important lesson about law school. He owned and managed a hidden rural place down by a creek, having a series of linked ponds each filled with progressively bigger fish, the last of which supplied grocers with farm-raised catch. On one of my visits, I asked him for his secret to success. Was it the cold water of the pristine creek, special fish feed he had developed, timed automatic feeding system he had designed, fancy aeration equipment, or close watch for fish disease? No, he shook his head, while smiling silently at a lawyer's piscicultural ignorance. He then motioned me toward a small dark hut jammed with fat white-plastic vats filled with thousands of tiny fish fry. "It's all in the size of the fry," he said. Seeing my continuing puzzlement, he explained, "Bigger fry, bigger fish." Light finally dawned: small baby fish grow into small adult fish, while big fry become big fish. Where you start makes a difference to where you finish. When you come to law school better prepared, you get through law school with more success.

You and every other new law student begin law school from your own starting points. Yes, you can learn in law school everything that you need to know about law, at least when law professors and deans design curriculum and instruction for optimal learning. The great majority of law graduates who take a bar exam pass a bar exam. No matter at what point you start law school, if you get in to an accredited law school, then you can learn enough law to pass the bar, obtain a law license, and help clients. Yet few if any law students want to just barely scrape by. Law school is an opportunity to fulfill to the greatest possible degree your learning potential, indeed the most meaningful and exciting intellectual program available anywhere. You can and should do more than just get by. So why not prepare even just a little for law school? Time and again, law professors see that students who start strong finish well ahead. Finishing well ahead doesn't just mean better grades and higher class standing. It can mean deeper, richer, more-useful law knowledge making for greater capability to practice law productively and effectively in a satisfying career. Take the following practical steps now to prepare for law school.

A. Health

Confirm your good diet, sleep, and exercise habits in the last few months and weeks before starting law school. If you can help it, then don't start physically out of shape or mentally stressed or exhausted. Your physical condition affects your mental acuity and well-being. Sometimes, one of the best things that you can do to improve your studies while in law school is to get in a physical workout, restoring your mental energy and emotional outlook. Starting law school physically fit can encourage you to stay fit through law school and into your career. If you need to quit smoking, or quit or reduce alcohol consumption, or give up certain unhealthy foods or other habits, then do so now (or at least take now the first steps toward doing so), before starting law school. If you haven't had a physical or dental exam in too long a time, or need to check your vision, or need other medical tests or care, then do those things now rather than once you start law school. The confidence, habits, and skills that law school promotes can change for the better your physical bearing, appearance, and demeanor. Begin that process of self-reflection and self-improvement now, even before you start law school.

B. Circumstances

Get your literal and figurative house in order before you start law school. Confirm that you have convenient, safe, secure, and affordable housing. Some law students start school without appropriate housing, while still in hotel rooms, or sleeping on a friend's or classmate's couch, or even sleeping in and living out of their car. Those students, while admirable for their flexibility and persistence, face burdens and challenges that you would rather avoid. If you are changing locations to start law school, then allow time to make and implement housing plans if you can. Whether you buy, borrow, or beg housing, ensure that you have a quiet place to study at home. If you expect to have roommates and have any choice, then choose law or medical students who, like you, will want abundant peace and quiet. Prefer proximity to your law school, or reliable transportation to and from school with a short commute, if you can. Longer commutes waste valuable time, although commutes on public transportation enabling you to study or in a vehicle where you can listen to class and other recordings can reduce lost time. If you need to repair or replace a vehicle to ensure reliable transportation, then try to do so before starting law school. Getting your financial affairs in order, such as ensuring that you have a local bank or other convenient access to funds and transaction services, can at times be critical. Balance your checkbook now. Resolve financial, contractual, and other legal disputes now, as far as you are able, so that they don't distract you later when you need study time.

C. Relationships

Also consider how you can best manage your roles and maintain your relationships before you start law school. If you are married or have a significant other, then discuss your planned class and study schedule with your partner, ensuring both that you have adequate time for study *and* that your partner has adequate time with you. Encourage your partner to attend any family-and-friends orientation that your law school offers or to review equivalent online or print materials. Allocate chores fairly

39

in advance rather than arguing about them later, which is always a good idea but can be especially helpful in preserving your concentration and mental energies for study rather than conflict resolution. If you have responsibility for children, then give sound advance consideration to how best to fulfill those responsibilities. Successful law students go through law school with kids of all ages or even having new kids (yes, more than one while in law school). Your children, though, should benefit from, not suffer from, law school. Share your childcare responsibilities with your spouse, other family members, and childcare professionals when able, but fulfill your responsibilities, too. Schedule family time if you must do so to ensure that your family members have your undivided energies and attention. At the same time, help them to understand the significance of your study time, not just to you but also to them. *Free lifetime legal service* is the humorous way (with a grain of truth) that family members may learn to respect your study time. Families benefit many ways from having as members well-compensated, respected lawyer professionals. Help your friends understand your new commitment to studies, too. You will make new friends in law school, but keeping old friends can be a very good thing, too.

D. Places

Locate and then prepare a good place for studying. That place may well be at home, unless home has too many distractions such as family members, friends, food, or entertainment options. You may instead need to make a law school location, library location, or coffeehouse your preferred study location, or move those locations around depending on day, time, and season. Law schools have carrels and conference rooms dedicated to student study use, even spaces that you can reserve. You may even decide to join or lead a student organization, one benefit of which may be access to an organization office that becomes your study space. In any case, your study-space criteria should include not only reducing distractions but also internet access and appropriate furniture, lighting, temperature, and other conditions. Furniture would include a desk-chair combination with electrical power for laptop computer and also soft, comfortable seating. Periodically moving from desk to soft seating and back again can reduce physical strain and increase study hours. Good lighting is important and good *natural* lighting better. Be conscious of lighting's secondary effects on mood and energy, such as with seasonal-affective disorder. Acquire study aids like a whiteboard and large paper on pad and easel or to tape to the wall. Collect stapler, tape, paper clips, post-it notes, and highlighters. Arrange these items in an orderly manner and visible and accessible location to give you an immediate sense of support and control. Make your study place appear and operate as a command center reflecting your commitment to success. You will draw surprising energy and assurance from doing so.

E. Technology

Confirm that you will have access to the internet through a reliable desktop or laptop computer or other device with which you can download, draft, and upload documents. Law schools, like undergraduate programs, use online course-management programs from which you can access syllabi, exercises, outlines, links, and other resources. Your ability to do so is critical to your success. Your law school will have a computer lab and print capability available to you. You need not bring your own device into the classroom or even have your own computer at all. Many law students and lawyers rely primarily on smartphones, tablets, notebook computers, or similar highly portable devices. An inexpensive laptop computer may well suffice. Law practice does not generally require the computing power of other professional work such as design, engineering, and finance, involving substantial number-crunching, modeling, or animation. You must, though, be ready to develop your technology skills. If you have a computer or other device but are unsure of its effectiveness for law school, then consider waiting until you start law school to determine whether you need to upgrade. Your law school technology staff and classmates will help you determine your technology needs. Don't waste financial resources on a fancy

41

computer before you start, especially when the technology may well be out of date already when you graduate.

F. Knowledge

Preparation also has a lot to do with the subject of law itself. Reading this book while reflecting on its exercises will help you prepare academically for law school, including helping you assess where you stand now before you start. The law readings and exercises in the following sections will remind you of law-related concepts that you have already learned while teaching you additional foundational law knowledge. You will also see forms of legal analysis, and law-practice constructs, that you will soon learn more deeply in law school and later use frequently in law practice. This book is your head start to grasp the law knowledge that the first year of law school teaches you, develop strong law-practice skills that law school's second year emphasizes, and connect your law studies with meaningful law-practice opportunities in law school's third year. Reflect on and complete each of the exercises at the end of each of the following sections. Get feedback on your answers from professors at the law school that you plan on attending. Get started early. Get started now. Remember: big fry, big fish.

Study. How prepared do you feel for law school? Given unlimited time and resources, a sound law school program could in theory make a lawyer out of just about anyone who is capable of academic studies. Many law students start law school with virtually no law knowledge, having come from medical, financial, engineering, or other backgrounds and educational programs. Yet time and resources are limited, and you surely want to make the most of your law school experience rather than find it to be a constant struggle. Rate yourself on a scale from 1 (unprepared) to 5 (highly prepared) in each of the following areas, the last several of which the following sections address in detail: (1) physical health; (2) mental health; (3) housing; (4) finances; (5) relationships; (6) knowledge of the law profession; (7) knowledge of law sources; (8) knowledge of law institutions; and (9) knowledge of law systems.

VII. What Is Legal Method?

Lawyer Skills. The American Bar Association's MacCrate Report long ago identified for legal education several core skills of lawyers. The foundation for lawyer skills involves determining client objectives, generating options for clients, and solving client problems. Law is a service profession. The work of lawyers is fundamentally purposeful, helping others achieve lawful goals. To achieve client goals, though, lawyers must be able to identify, research, analyze, and resolve legal issues. They must also investigate facts, obtain information and evidence, and prove fact issues. Yet these fundamental lawyer skills are not enough. To be effective in their client service, lawyers must also be able to counsel clients while communicating clearly and advocating effectively both orally and in writing. Lawyers should also be able to negotiate, litigate, and use other alternative dispute resolution. Finally, lawyers must be able to manage client relationships and the enterprise of law practice, all within ethical bounds. These MacCrate Report skills include both cognitive (thinking) and affective (doing) skills. Consider first the cognitive skills.

A. Thinking as Lawyers

Reasoning as Core Skill. Lawyers use highly effective reasoning skills. Experts in all fields reason critically, developing cognitive structures and protocols to guide their practice. Lawyers, though, concentrate their expert reasoning around social problems. While other professions place medicine, finance, buildings, products, technology, theology, or other subjects at the center of their professional practice, lawyers place critical

45

reasoning itself at the core, with the whole of human enterprise arrayed around it. Lawyer reasoning skill fascinates not so much because of the effectiveness of the skill itself but because of the fundamentally humane purposes for which lawyers employ the skill. Lawyer skills are common even if acutely concentrated, while their goal is general, imperative, and divine.

Cognition. To become an effective lawyer, you must learn law's knowledge base in useable form. Law is action logic, meant for use. The quality of a lawyer's thinking determines the quality of the lawyer's service. This part introduces some of the cognitive skills lawyers use in providing legal services. Make no effort to memorize these skills. Simply recognize them while thinking through the exercises accompanying each section. Law school will demonstrate these skills repeatedly, giving you plenty of opportunity to practice them. Begin with basic mental processing before considering forms of reasoning and discerning. Appreciate law school's power as an investment in your mind.

Processing. Lawyers process substantial information in order to form sound judgments and give sound advice. Lawyers read, review, skim, and glean written information efficiently. They also listen effectively. Yet lawyers do not simply read and listen as others read and listen. Rather, as lawyers read and listen, lawyers turn quantities of information into helpful accounts, patterns, and constructs to test those constructs against law's rules, definitions, and frameworks. Law school helps you learn to think with energy, clarity, and consistency that you have never before maintained. Follow practices that promote your mental health and energy. Exercising several times improves your mental energy. A good diet and adequate sleep help maintain mental energy. Reduce stress by eliminating procrastination and over-commitment, and restoring life balance. Leave room for creativity. Be curious. Enjoy each subject, and above all, explore.

Focus. Emotions and relationships are other important factors influencing your ability to think and learn. Trust, respect, and appreciate your professors and classmates. Maintain good relationships. Monitor and control your emotions. Promptly address situations that interfere with clear thinking. Appreciate that others will think and act differently. Do not expect to experience and overcome the same challenges as your classmate, in the same way, by the same means, in the same time. Expect differences. Do one thing at a time. Do not study law while watching television, listening to the radio, or holding conversations. Studies show that multi-tasking is really performing separate tasks reducing your productivity while increasing errors. Expect your focus to lapse. Use movement and emotion to regain focus. Use more of your senses as you study. When reading, speak important phrases to activate your aural and oral senses. When listening, take notes and draw diagrams to activate your kinesthetic and visual senses. Move your hands and change your expression and posture as you speak.

Memory. Memory is important to lawyer thinking. You need not have a superior memory. You should learn ways to remember. Memory involves three mental operations: (1) encoding, which is to read, see, or hear in a way that enables grasp or understanding; (2) storing, which is to connect the encoded information with existing mental frameworks; and (3) retrieving, which is to access and recall the encoded and stored information. Encoding is often automatic as you read, see, or listen, although some memories like those necessary for legal analysis you must encoded with effort. You must concentrate to attach more meaning to what you read, see, or hear. Storing involves elaboration, that you mull and manipulate the encoded information until it connects with already-existing memories. To increase storage and retrieval, repeat new information at short and long intervals. Review immediately after learning and again later.

Reading. Law texts are different from what you usually read. Lawyers read law texts differently. You must follow different strategies and use different methods to read law productively. Law students who use these different strategies and methods have greater academic success. You must consistently step beyond the text. First discern why you are reading the text—to learn what

47

aspect of what subject? Then connect that subject to what you have already learned. Where does the reading fit with what you already know? Then, as you read, raise and answer questions about the text. Read for curiosity, interest, inspiration, education, and advocacy. Law students who exhibit greater internal motivation of these kinds perform better while being more satisfied and less anxious. Develop and maintain a strong sense of humanity, compassion, commitment, and identity, even while you learn the analysis typically associated with law. See the humanity in your law reading, even as you learn the formal skills of law.

Reading Cases. In our common-law tradition, cases are the fundamental units of law. A case presents as an account between interested parties. The case opinion that you read addresses and resolves the conflict in the parties' interests. Lawyers use case opinions to argue for outcomes in subsequent cases. Lawyers do not read cases for plot, characters, theme, or literary technique, as you learned or may prefer to read. Lawyers instead read cases to apply case rules or holdings to their own cases. Thus when reading a case, a lawyer first identifies the issue the case addresses and then the rule or holding of the case. The lawyer also discerns the case's critical facts to see how like or unlike the facts of the lawyer's own case. Lawyers also explore the rationale that the case opinion used to decide the issue including any authority on which the opinion relied. Similarly, law students learn first to read a single case for a clear rule or holding, then multiple cases for a framework or synthesis of a law subject. Law students then learn to read a single case for unresolved issues before finally reading multiple cases for trends or tendencies within the law.

Approach. So when you read cases in law school, think first about the purpose of your reading. Examine the course syllabus and chapter and subchapter headings. Connect the case with the subject you are learning. Determine why the casebook authors chose this particular case. Second, read for an overview of the case. Discern the opinion's general structure. Look at the start for a procedural summary and statement of the issue. Learn why the opinion is necessary, meaning what law issue it addresses. Then grasp the fact setting. Know what happened to whom for what reason. Then discern who won in the case opinion and the rule of law that caused the win. Identify the authority for the rule, whether constitutional, statutory, regulatory, or common law. Look for any analysis, rationale, or reasoning.

Analysis. Read cases analytically. Distinguish relevant from irrelevant facts, and identify the one or two critical facts. Watch for qualifying terms like *if, when, unless, until,* and *only*. Ask how the opinion defines key terms and phrases. Determine the opinion's rationale, whether straightforward application of authority or nuanced policy decision. If the opinion followed authority, then ask whether the authority was new or old, uniform or disputed, and sound or unsound. If the opinion relied on policy rationales, then ask what interests justified the policy, and whether the policy's grounds were empirically true or provable. Ask whether the decision was fair, equitable, proportional, fitting, and moral. Consider whether the decision was something that legislatures rather than courts should make. Consider also whether you agree or disagree with the case holding and outcome. Most of all, determine how the case fits into your learning. Synthesize the case with other cases into your subject framework. Decide whether the case illustrates the rule or an exception to the rule, a majority or minority rule, and an extension of the law or confirmation of settled law. Hypothesize other applications of the case. Decide whom you would rather represent and why.

Concepts. Law practice is intellectual. Lawyers work with concepts. A concept represents objects, acts, events, processes, and other things in ways readily understood by others. To *know* a law concept means that you can recall it from memory, explain it to another, give examples and non-examples of it, and recognize when the concept applies to something you encounter in law practice. Lawyers are expert analysts because of their ability to acquire, recall, and use concepts that represent larger commitments and meanings. Learn to use mental images and shorthand symbols to help recall more-complex concepts.

Lawyers are expert at analysis because of their ability to recall and use meaning-laden words. Images, words, and symbols aid recall. Your ability to form and recall concepts improves with practice. While you learn law, you develop and improve your methods of learning law. Lawyers are expert learners.

Frameworks. After identifying concepts, your law school success depends on your skill at organizing frameworks out of those concepts. Lawyers use mental frameworks as procedural protocols when analyzing law issues. Lawyers often use the basic IRAC framework to represent legal analysis. Lawyers begin by identifying the issue, then state the law or rule, then test facts against the law in an analysis, and finally reach a conclusion — together, Issue, Rule, Analysis, and Conclusion, or IRAC. Lawyers follow other frameworks peculiar to their specific law field. Some frameworks reflect the substantive law while others they use as procedural devices. Frameworks help you organize, recall, and use law concepts. Lawyers continually confirm, expand, and modify their law frameworks. With your professors' help, and through activities like reviewing and outlining, you will gradually develop law frameworks. Lawyers are expert at assembling and using frameworks to recall and apply law in different areas.

Example Framework. Take as an example a framework that law students usually learn early in their first term. Your Torts studies will help you learn the concept of *knowing the substantial certainty of harm*. For convenience's sake, you can label this new concept with the symbol KSC (Knowledge of Substantial Certainty). You also learn that knowledge of substantial certainty of harm is one of three ways, along with the desire to harm (DH) and transferred intent (TI), to satisfy the intent (I) element of a battery (B) claim. You also learn that a battery claim has the not only the element of intent but also of harm or offense (HO), and victim contact (C). Battery is just one of five traditional intentional torts along with assault (A), false imprisonment (FI), trespass to land (TL), and trespass to chattels (TC). These several concepts form a simple framework as follows:

IT

☐

A, B, FI, TL, TC

☐

I, HO, C

☐

DH, KSC, TI

Reasoning. Critical reasoning means for you to allow sound conceptual and ethical bases that you are able to articulate, rather than personality, prejudice, power, chance, or other non-rational conditions, guide your conclusions. Lawyers depend on critical reasoning. Critical reasoning enables lawyers to promote peace, prosperity, justice, and liberty within democratic and principled order. Critical reasoning is normative, working in ways that Americans generally accept as fitting for private action and public governance. The ability to reason in a wide variety of social contexts is largely what distinguishes lawyers from non-lawyer decision-makers. Societies that do not have a high percentage of citizens capable of and committed to reason's movement, and indeed do not have a class of lawyer professionals highly trained in reason, will not be stable and orderly societies promoting individual and public welfare. Unreasoned decisions are disastrous not merely for individuals and families but also for communities, states, and nations, in regional and national land-use planning, markets and finance, transportation and manufacturing, business formation and governance, labor and human resources, and a host of other fields. The ability of large numbers of lawyers to evaluate critically is essential to the welfare of the American nation.

Learned Reasoning. We learn reasoning rather than possess it innately. Reasoning means thinking in a manner different from the way in which people ordinarily think. To develop reasoning skills, you must do something out of the ordinary. Law school's first year helps you learn to reason in the professional context in which lawyers practice. Critical reasoning does not consider the cause for a person's position or the person's merit or identity. The critical thinker cares little about who made the statement or what caused them to make it. Critical reasoning instead considers a statement's content rather than its source or cause. Critical thinkers consider grounds or reasons for agreeing or disagreeing with assertions. Challenging an assertion as unreasoned is no offense to its author, just as justifying a statement is not the author's endorsement. Unreasoned thought treats an assertion as if within a closed system, questioning only what caused or who made the assertion. Reasoned thought instead treats statements as if within open systems, considering wide grounds supporting or challenging the assertion, while articulating different possible goals, purposes, policies, interests, and meanings.

Deduction. Reasoning has two main forms, deduction and induction. Classically, deduction involves stating a major premise followed by a minor premise followed by a conclusion, as in if A=B (major premise) and B=C (minor premise), then A=C (conclusion). The question of whether the facts of a case satisfy the elements of a civil tort or criminal charge depends largely on deductive reasoning. The element's definition is the major premise, the available facts are the minor premise, and articulating whether the facts satisfy the element is the conclusion. Deductive reasoning requires drawing conclusions from logic, rule, definition, condition, or other principle. If law presents a continuum from clear rules at one end ("no vessel sails without one life preserver for each person on board") to vague standards at the other end ("all vessels must maintain reasonably safe conditions"), then deductive reasoning occurs nearer the rule end of the continuum.

Induction. By contrast, inductive reasoning lies at the *vague standards* end of the rules-standard spectrum. Inductive reasoning involves assembling information into useful patterns or conclusions. You might examine case materials to draw relevant facts illustrating significant features of the event. Or you might examine a collection of cases from which you draw the law or rule for your case. Assembling the facts of a case or reading a series of cases for a rule are both inductive processes. Inductive processes like developing a case theme or articulating disputed law require skill, experience, and perspective, can be more personal and creative than deduction, and draw on wider sources. While the plain logic of deductive reasoning attracts the reasoned thinker like the lawyer or judge, juries may respond more readily to inductive statements. Watch a skilled trial lawyer reconstruct events into a compelling case. Inductive reasoning is enormously powerful and valuable.

Inference. Lawyers also exercise strong inferential-reasoning skills. To infer is to suppose that a condition may exist from the existence of other closely related matters. Inference is not logic but supposition. Inference produces error. Just because a driver crossing the centerline follows from the driver's being drunk does not mean that drunkenness always occurs with crossing the centerline. Crossing the centerline may have several other causes like sleepiness or cellphone use. Yet conjecturing the possibility of drunkenness would encourage a lawyer to investigate. Lawyers are good at inferential reasoning because they deal constantly with unknown facts and uncertain circumstances. Lawyers must have the skill of thinking of what the facts might be, to be able to make reasonable requests for evidence of them.

Generalizing. Lawyers must constantly generalize situations and decisions for rules to apply to their own current cases. The common law arises out of a mass of individual decisions. Judicial opinions decide specific cases on certain facts. Lawyers must generalize their holdings to apply to their own cases. You learn to generalize rules by reading series of cases. Generalizing rules can be as simple as substituting a broader class or category of items or actions for the specific item or action in the original case, substituting broad for narrow terms. You must simply learn to make reasonable judgments as to what to generalize. The skill of recognizing what generalizations to make and not make is one that you can expect to take years to master.

Applying. Lawyers simultaneously narrow general rules so as to determine whether they apply to their specific cases. You must develop the skill of phrasing rules in more specific terms to apply to your situation. For example, tort law provides that one who violates a safety statute suffers an inference of negligence, meaning carelessness. So then, to apply the general rule to a specific situation, speeding is usually careless. Yet not always. A law-enforcement officer who speeds after a fleeing felon and an ambulance driver who speeds to the hospital with a dying patient are not necessarily careless. You must think of the safety statute's purpose (to keep the general flow of traffic to a safe speed) and consider the circumstances (the need to save or protect lives) to know whether the specific application of the general rule is valid. Lawyers must judge whether a rule applies to a situation.

Evaluating. Clients most appreciate their lawyers for using these analytic skills to evaluate their matters. To have a discerning professional in one's corner can make an enormous difference to the future of an individual, family, business, institution, and community. To discern is to perceive and articulate solutions and truths that others do not see, to understand and judge discriminately. Lawyers evaluate all manner of matters including legal rights, solutions, arguments, options, approaches, arrangements, relationships, and compromises. Lawyers identify assertions and then evaluate those assertions using analytic skill. Is the assertion something that the lawyer can and should support? Answering that question requires that the lawyer be a skilled evaluator. Lawyers are constantly recognizing and testing premises. They recognize assumptions, looking for suppositions that may not be true. They recognize relevant evidence making an assertion more or less likely, recognizing consistency and inconsistency between evidence and assertion, and when evidence is sufficient to support an assertion. Lawyers know when to draw inferences from that evidence. They know how to draw conclusions while also knowing the implications of conclusions.

Uncertainty. Given the complex, varied, and shifting circumstances in which we live and relate to one another, a lawyer's practice of applying law to facts is inherently uncertain. Lawyers recognize uncertainty as important and useful. The language of lawyers is therefore both ambiguous and precise. Lawyers carefully qualify their conclusions to measure and quantify uncertainty. Law, while rule-based, also has historical and social relativity. Legal reasoning is not merely formal but dialectical, meaning a back-and-forth proposition. Ambiguity creates room for reflection, to adjust arguments to recognize new and competing interests and needs. Uncertainty creates the opportunity if not the need for compromise. It leaves room to incorporate others' views while expanding options and possibilities. Ambiguity is the gap through which lawyers make their clients real to others to deal more sensitively with their humanity. Ambiguity prevents authorities from manipulating formal rules in harsh, prejudicial, and destructive manner.

Precision. Despite uncertainty, a lawyer's analysis is also precise, using specific verbal formulations to represent specific constructs. If law had no necessary constructs, such as claims, charges, elements, conditions, and criteria, then parties would have nothing around which to structure uncertainties. If law were entirely relative, then lawyers would be unable to arrive at common meanings, support compromise, and achieve resolution. Lawyers precisely analyze each law construct, shaping their arguments around those constructs to reflect both the precision of law but also the variety of circumstance and uncertainty of outcome. Experienced lawyers and judges, and inexperienced lawyers who are astute enough to find databases, reports, and other sources for experience, use that combination of precision and uncertainty to reflect their wisdom.

Hypothesizing. To test the validity and reliability of their reasoning, lawyers also employ hypothetical fact scenarios. Ethics rules and moral sensibility prohibit lawyers from knowingly using false evidence. Yet lawyers hypothesize facts for several legitimate purposes. One reason has to do with discovering unknown facts. A lawyer's ability to hypothesize possible or probable facts leads to investigation to confirm or contradict those possibilities. Lawyers must also anticipate facts and circumstances that have not yet occurred, to help clients plan for future events and contingencies, such as when drafting contracts, forming business organizations, or conveying property. Even when events have already occurred and the parties agree on what happened, lawyers may hypothesize other facts in order to fully appreciate the significance of the known facts. Hypothetical scenarios help lawyers make informed judgments about the matter at hand. Judges will even write opinions using contrasting scenarios as to the knowledge and experience of the involved individuals, deliberateness or reprehensibility of their acts, harm or lack of harm to the victim, the degree of risk associated with the conduct, and any number of other circumstances.

Scaling. You can improve your contrasting of hypothetical scenarios by scaling them along a spectrum or continuum, from exaggerated contrasting points at either end. Where a case presents a range of possible outcomes falling within or outside of a law rule, a conceptual continuum aids your analysis. You place the actual case fact and hypothetical scenarios along the rule's continuum, nearer or farther from or the other end, to justify conclusions. Any one case may involve several alternative conceptual fields, perhaps around duties owed, or the nature and reprehensibility of their breaches, or the foreseeability of the risks, and so on. Experienced lawyers construct and use these mental scales to evaluate and argue cases. You, too, should recognize and use scaling as another form of reasoning. Be ready to construct an appropriate conceptual field and place your case facts within it.

Conditions. Many legal claims or charges have *elements*, which are individual conditions for the claim or charge to prevail. Lawyers discover evidence, evaluate claims, and present their cases using the elements of the claim or charge as the organizing framework. Evidence satisfies an element or condition when a reasonable person could so conclude. To determine whether evidence satisfies an element, you must first know how the law defines the element. An element may have a definition or list of criteria to help a lawyer determine when the evidence satisfies the element. Defining an element is not the same as determining whether evidence satisfies the element. To determine whether evidence satisfies an element requires linking the element's definition with the case facts. Lawyers compare and contrast the facts with the definition to see if the facts fall within the definition. If the facts meet the element's definition or criteria, then the evidence has satisfied the element. Although satisfying an element may sound logical and scientific, in many cases the lawyers and parties cannot conclude with any certainty, increasing the significance of evaluation and advocacy.

Factors. The law does not determine all rights and claims using elements. In some instances, proving a claim or satisfying one of its elements require weighing evidence against a list of factors. Factors differ from elements. Elements are conditions, each of which must be satisfied. Factors are considerations that, by their accumulation or weight, tend to make the proof of a claim or element more or less likely. Evidence need not satisfy all factors. Evidence may support some factors but not others. Factors also need not be exclusive. The law may permit you to add other factors. While some factors may be more important than others, no one factor is necessary. Weighing factors begins with identifying the factor, equating case facts as bearing weight for or against the factor, and concluding which side the factor favors. Weighing factors is a common analytic skill for lawyers.

Study. You represent a teacher accused of having committed a civil battery on a student struck by a potato shot from a pressurized tube in the teacher's science demonstration. Explain in writing to your client whether the student's civil battery claim satisfies the elements of intent, harm or offense, and contact. Next, review your answer, counting how many of the above analytic skills you used. Consider supplementing your answer to increase the number of those skills.

B. Working as Lawyers

Research. Those who have not practiced law might guess that research is a lawyer's primary skill. They would not be far wrong. Lawyers first must know when they need to research. While lawyers learn and retain much law knowledge, they also constantly encounter issues requiring research into new law. Lawyers then plan for that research, discerning the likely sources of authority and the search terms and approach. They then implement those plans (do the research) using a variety of print media and electronic services, software, and databases. Lawyers then assess their research progress against timelines and goals, and modify their plans to respond to their assessment. They also monitor law changes that might affect the accuracy of their reported research results. Research is a critical skill and engaging activity for many practitioners, all of whom will have learned the skill.

Writing. Lawyers memorialize their research results in court briefs, office memoranda, client correspondence, and other forms. They draft and write constantly for many other reasons. Lawyers first identify the need for written work product and discern the purpose of those writings. They then plan document form and structure. They then do the drafting, whether of court pleadings, motions, and briefs, or client correspondence, contracts, corporate articles and bylaws, wills, or other legal documents. Their writing must be precise, understandable, and clear. Lawyers adjust their writing to their audiences, whether appellate judges who expect the finest writing skill and deepest thought, trial judges who expect clarity and brevity, opposing counsel who expect civility and respect, or clients who expect writing that they can understand and that gets to the point. Lawyers also know how to execute, route, and store those writings. If lawyers could choose just one strong skill, then many would choose writing.

Interviewing. Lawyers represent clients. The nation's economy depends on private rights. Individuals and the corporate entities that they create and manage need law services to survive, participate, and prosper within that vast system of private rights. The need for law services means obtaining and accepting the services of a lawyer. Lawyer-client relationships begin with an interview, whether in the lawyer's office or client's home, a hospital room, jail or prison, homeless shelter, courthouse, or coffee shop. Lawyers interview clients and others to obtain the information and establish the relationships through which they will provide effective legal services. Lawyers are good at interviewing. A successful interview depends on preparation. Lawyers discern interview purposes and anticipate interview opportunities. They practice strong listening and communication skills, asking open-ended questions to generate trust, demonstrate compassion, and acquire information, and close-ended questions to guide, control, and conclude the interview. They recognize, adapt, and adjust to others' communication preferences. Watching a skilled lawyer prepare for, perform, and conclude an interview will convince anyone that interviewing is a hugely valuable and richly complex skill.

Documenting Action. Lawyers also know how to document interview outcomes and take action. Lawyers prepare fee agreements and dictate and draft client and insurer summaries, and file memoranda, to keep everyone informed of status and information. Even as interviews proceed, lawyers develop action items such as records to obtain, others to interview or depose, requests or demands to make, and counts or defenses to plead. To conclude an interview, a lawyer will confirm with the client steps that the lawyer and legal assistant will take to further the client's matter, and get client approval and authorizations. Lawyer and client will agree on communication protocol for the form and frequency of updates on the lawyer's actions and information. The lawyer will then take prompt action to schedule work and assign tasks to subordinate lawyers or staff. A lawyer's law knowledge is action logic. Law practice entails movement, initiative, and momentum, constantly communicated and documented.

Counseling. Lawyers are also counselors. The phrase *Attorney and Counselor at Law* appears on lawyer business cards, letterhead, signs, and other marketing. In their advocacy, lawyers engage those who have the authority and discretion to affect client matters. In their counsel, lawyers pour their insight, energy, and encouragement into the client relationship. They help clients discern goals, objectives, interests, options, and outcomes. They help clients see opportunities and challenges. Primarily, though, lawyers help clients better see their own situation, how their actions, reputation, and character affect their prospects and relationships. Lawyers also help clients prioritize interests and evaluate options so that clients can direct their energy into the most fruitful matters. Lawyers respect client autonomy. Lawyers do not make decisions for and control their clients. Yet lawyers also do more than simply strategize with clients over legal matters. Lawyers constantly communicate with their clients in ways that affect positively their clients' futures. Lawyers give not only legal but also moral, financial, political, and social counsel. Lawyers know that law problems and opportunities lie within other interests. Lawyers communicate how legal issues affect the client's job, family, community, and future. Clients retain lawyers as much for their wise counsel as for other legal service.

Investigation. Lawyers also investigate, employing skills that satisfy curiosity and inform lawyers about surprising human propensities. Truth is stranger than fiction. Lawyers retain and work closely with private investigators, police officers, medical examiners, professionals who reconstruct accidents, and other experts who gather, interpret, and testify as to evidence. Lawyers recognize when they need to investigate, what form investigation should take, and to what use to put the information investigation generates. Lawyers plan and budget for investigation. They identify what evidence they need to prove or defend claims, and determine lawful means to obtain that evidence even when adversaries plan that they not do so. Lawyers deploy several forms of discovery that court rules and procedures permit, like depositions (oral examination under oath before a court reporter), interrogatories (written questions that must be answered under oath), and document requests. They subpoena individuals to appear, testify, and produce records, and gather electronic evidence. Once lawyers obtain evidence, they evaluate its reliability and relevance. Investigation is a fascinating process of reconstructing client events, experiences, and circumstances, in which lawyers are expert.

Negotiation. Lawyers are also negotiators and problem-solvers. Even in the most-contentious arenas with important rights and interests at stake, and indeed especially in those arenas, lawyers employ their negotiation skills to discern opportunities, foster compromise, and bring about resolution. Lawyers help articulate achievable client goals while helping clients recognize others' goals and interests. Lawyers know when and how to obtain client authority to negotiate and recognize when others have or do not have that authority. Lawyers know how to conduct negotiations using mediation, case evaluation, arbitration, and other methods. They help their clients choose favorable dispute-resolution forums. Lawyers know how to give and read the signals that opposing sides send to move negotiations forward without making unauthorized concessions or unwise disclosures. Lawyers are also expert at documenting settlement agreements to ensure that they bind consenting parties. Negotiation is a fascinating skill that lawyers exercise frequently, effectively, and wisely.

Confrontation. Lawyer reputations for contentiousness are due largely to lawyers being truth-tellers. To resolve conflict, lawyers must often compel parties to recognize events, actions, relationships, and interests that they would rather deny or ignore. Lawyers help others confront what they must confront to reach resolution. Lawyers confront others in ways that generate helpful change and peaceful resolution. Lawyers sometimes confront their own clients who need to acknowledge situations and change behaviors. Just as often, lawyers help clients confront their adversaries, not to foster conflict but to resolve it. Some conflicts one cannot and should not avoid because avoidance brings no resolution. Lawyers are expert at discerning when confrontation may be necessary and productive. They then know how to communicate in ways that simultaneously reveal and heal, like debriding wounds of infectious material. Value the confrontation skills of lawyers.

Litigation. Lawyers ultimately have the government's authority to invoke judicial procedures to compel others to do as they would rather not do. Parties litigate with the same conflict-resolution purpose that they negotiate. Lawyer skill is obviously critical to successful litigation. Lawyers know court rules and procedures. They know how to prepare, file, and serve pleadings and other court papers. They know how to acquire and offer evidence, and test an opposing party's evidence. Lawyers are expert in preparing jury instructions that state the law in simple and compelling terms. They know how to draft findings of fact and present and challenge proposed orders and judgments. Lawyers also know how to take appeals when trial judges err and judicial proceedings produce unjust outcomes. At each litigation stage, lawyers help the parties consider what the law requires of them, toward resolutions that restore and preserve peace while providing recovery, restitution, and redemption. Lawyers litigate not for show but for justice.

Management. While practicing the above skills, lawyers are also skilled managers. They manage client relationships, law firm finances, calendars, caseloads, court procedures, and conduct rules. They manage relationships with opposing counsel, co-counsel, and lawyers who appear before them or before whom they appear in mediations, arbitrations, and case evaluations. Lawyers use systems to increase their productivity and efficiency, and prioritize work. Although they often rely on legal assistants, secretaries, and administrative assistants, lawyers know how to maintain files and manage cases and projects. They develop and use templates, forms, checklists, and tools to measure, track, and assess caseloads and individual case progress. Lawyers record their work to bill fairly and efficiently for their services. They structure relationships and price services to treat clients equitably.

They meet law firm expectations for billable hours while simultaneously ensuring that each client receives full value for billed services.

Goals. Lawyers manage not primarily for their own benefit or that of their family and friends but for the benefit of client, firm, profession, and public. Lawyers also manage for personal wellness, balance, and mental, emotional, and physical health. Lawyers set broad professional goals such as to earn good reputation, increase specialty skills, broaden practice areas, and improve the justice system and profession. They plan intermediate objectives to reach those broad goals, such as to take continuing legal education, volunteer for bar committees, accept pro-bono assignments, and research and write for bar journals. Lawyers know to develop and implement marketing plans to ensure that the public knows the availability and value of their services. Lawyers have a professional competence about them unique to the law profession. Practicing law is among the most engaging, humane, and responsible of vocations. To become a practicing lawyer is to enter a venerated, noble, and immensely rewarding profession.

Study. You represent an employer whose terminated employee has notified of an impending employment-rights lawsuit. Your employer client hopes to resolve the anticipated litigation as quickly as possible to reduce the impact on budget and employee morale. Explain in writing to your client your plan to use the above skills to achieve the client's objective.

VIII. How Do I Learn?

Introduction

Forget for a moment that your challenge and opportunity are to learn *law*. Think for a moment about how you best learn *anything*. On its face, learning seems simple, something like a process in which you read, listen, think, know, recall, and use. In practice, though, effective learning involves many habits, practices, performances, routines, and skills. Law students don't learn differently. Sure, *what* you learn (law) is different from what you learned in an undergraduate program (political science, criminal justice, sociology, education, etc.) and what other graduate and professional students learn in programs like medicine, dentistry, accounting, engineering, nursing, social work, and so on. Yet *how* you learn law is very like how you learned in your undergraduate program and how other graduate students learn in medicine, dentistry, accounting, and so on. The main things that change from undergraduate programs to law school are instead the *quantity* of your learning, the *precision* of your learning, and the *performances* expected of you in clinical programs, licensure exams, and beyond in law practice. Consider, then, how various strategies, schedules, resources, performances, and behaviors can improve how you learn law.

A. Strategies

First, the large quantity of law that you will learn in law school together with the precise way in which lawyers use law knowledge indicate that you must become particularly knowledgeable and skilled to graduate from law school and pass

65

the bar exam. Study strategies thus matter in law school. How skilled you are studying and particularly at altering your study methods over time will go a long way toward how much you learn in law school. Your challenge is not simply learning a lot of law but also putting that law into practice in a sort of *action logic*. Law school helps you prepare not for a specific known matter but instead for *likely unknown* matters within multiple law fields. Your studies must therefore be programmatic, thoughtful, and deliberate if you are to avoid simply flailing away against a vast body of law while acquiring only poorly defined and ineffective skills. Consider a few helpful study strategies.

Tactics. Recognize when you are deploying one study tactic out of a range of available study tactics. Study tactics should change as each term progresses and as your law education progresses. Reading an assignment, taking notes as you read, and discussing the subject in and out of class are one set of tactics that may work well for understanding. Yet that tactical set won't do you much good for organizing, synthesizing, and recalling all aspects of the subject as the term progresses. Rather, a new tactical set involving review, outlining, and fluency trials with flashcards would likely synthesize the subject while increasing the speed and accuracy of your recall. Yet that second tactical set won't do you enough good for the actual performance expected of you in each subject, whether the performance involves quickly answering many multiple-choice questions, writing short essays analyzing hypothetical scenarios, negotiating a dispute resolution, or arguing a motion in a mock court hearing. You would need instead to alter your tactical set to practice the performance with feedback. Your ability and willingness to modify tactics as you proceed is a key strategy that largely determines your study effectiveness.

Goals. Adopting and pursuing goals is another effective study strategy. Set goals that challenge and inspire you, not ones that imply mere survival. If your only goal in a course is to pass, then you may do so, barely. If instead your goal is to ace the course, then your goal may substantially increase your likelihood

66

of passing. Yet don't simply set external goals that the school requires of you. Instead, set internal goals such as to master a subject, evidenced by such externals as the professor's recommendation letter, a research or teaching-assistant role, or a certificate of merit or scholarship. While setting high but achievable goals for courses, terms, and years, also set monthly, weekly, and daily objectives. When you set an objective for the day's preparation such as to complete review of a certain subject and then practice a certain number of multiple-choice and essay questions at a certain performance level, you will naturally organize your activities for the day toward accomplishing that objective. Set frequent small goals that daily move you closer to your larger goals. Increasing the frequency with which you face immediate necessary sub-goals helps you avoid the procrastination, fear, and frustration that can arise from looking only at your distant overall goal. Consistent daily progress on sub-goals will give you the sense of accomplishment necessary to sustain your overall studies at a high level over time.

Effort. Another effective study strategy is to deploy maximum effort, engaging your mind, body, and emotions to the fullest. Study shows that *work drive* correlates with law school (and other!) success. Develop a passion for law studies. Immerse yourself in law's power, purpose, and subtle beauty. Your satisfaction and success in a law or law-related career will depend on how much you care about what you are doing. Don't hesitate to strive and even to struggle in order to grasp the subject of your studies through substantial effort. Take each new day as an opportunity to accomplish something new and worthwhile through focused effort. Study sessions are both more effective and more efficient when you engage the subject with full effort. While the quantity of your effort in some way counts, do not assume that simply putting in large numbers of hours in bar preparation will lead to success. Don't let your attitude be one of drudgery. Instead, put in *productive*, not unproductive, hours. Avoid the idea that if your studies are easy, then they are

67

effective. To retain your newfound law knowledge, you should rehearse it actively with full effort.

Assess. Another effective study strategy is to count, record, measure, and monitor your performance. Choose goals and sub-goals that you can measure. Then use those measurements to guide your study tactics, focus, and effort. Using data to make decisions is a key strategy for professionals in many fields. Count and record anything that might help you improve your performance. What one counts gets one's attention. Simply by counting and recording your performances will tend to turn your mind and energy to improving those performances. Completing one day or one week of studies that seemed vaguely productive does not mean that you should repeat the same activity. Instead, look at whether you met your sub-goals. Project the next performance based on your current performance. Ask whether, if you keep progressing at your current rate, your studies will have prepared you for the final exam. If your rate of progress falls short, then change your study strategies. Measuring progress on frequent sub-goals gives you frequent opportunities to benchmark your performance gains against what you will need to achieve mastery. Save what works, while jettisoning what doesn't work. Make changes where you see opportunity for improvement. Expect low scores on your first practice tests, and expect to improve those scores with diligent and effective practice. Record, compare, and contrast your scores from practice test to practice test. Let your improvement encourage you to increase your studies and confirm the effectiveness of your study methods. Plan for improvement, and work for improvement. You can only know if you are making adequate progress when you measure and assess your performance. Be sure that your incremental gains are large enough to reach the goal.

Focus. Studying what you do *not* know rather than what you *do* know is another important strategy. Don't believe that you are learning best when feeling comfortable and confident about the subject. Learning requires mental discomfort as the mind forms and adjusts to new cognitive structures. Studying only what you already know may feel comfortable but will lull you into poor performance. Rather, challenge yourself to study what your practice and assessment shows that you *don't* know. If you are know every word of an outline or audio or video recording and are getting all of the answers right on your practice tests in one subject area, then force yourself to concentrate on other resources that you don't know and to practice tests on which you are not yet performing strongly. Don't waste precious time to make yourself feel good about what you already know. Instead, attack, struggle with, and master what you *don't* know. Performing masterfully in one area but abysmally in other areas is not a sensible option. Your strategy should be to develop comprehensive knowledge and skill so that you can perform competently in all areas even while masterfully in your strong areas. Show your knowledge and skill everywhere, not just here and there. Lawyers certainly specialize in practice, but the profession still generally requires broad basic competence. Lawyers should share a certain quantity and quality of professional knowledge and equal degrees of professional skill. Pursue comprehensive preparation rather than piecemeal excellence.

B. Schedules

Beyond your specific study strategies, you should also make good use of your available time. Law school requires that you devote substantial time to studying. You will not find enough time for law school among your usual activities. You will need more time than small schedule adjustments will allow. Most of us are poor judges of how much time we need to allocate for major commitments. We tend to be overly optimistic, only to find ourselves short of the necessary hours, days, or weeks we need to complete a task. A few tips can help you overcome such planning errors. First, look backwards for help in crafting your time estimates. Look at how often you found your studies interrupted by others. Learn to include the time that unplanned interruptions tend to consume. Another tip is to estimate study time based on individual components rather than study as a whole. Calculate your final estimate by adding up the time expected for each of the individual study activities. You may be surprised at how much more time you need in contrast to your estimate based on the overall study subject alone. Then, devote to studying the time that you set aside to do so. Don't simply schedule study time. Use scheduled time for studies.

Awareness. Learn to become aware of what you are doing whenever you are doing it. Lawyers and other professionals acquire a constant sense of the value of their current activity toward the professional objective that they are trying to achieve. We constantly measure the worth of what we are doing against the purpose that we have for doing it. Law school trains law students in similar time valuing. If you enjoy aimlessness, then law school is not the time to pursue that pleasure. Recognize when you are using time well and when you are not. You need not study every minute, but you do need to know generally when you are advancing in your studies and when you are not. Consider creating an electronic calendar or purchasing a paper calendar solely for your law studies. Record detailed day-to-day study plans and their implementation. Use your calendar to build in frequent sub-goals in advance, adjusting the sub-goals as needed according to the results of your measurement and assessment. Get study plans in your mind and then on your calendar. Be especially thoughtful and intentional about specific activities on specific dates. If you find yourself procrastinating, then consider choosing someone to help you meet your study goals. Devise positive consequences for meeting your goals and negative consequences for not meeting them. Highly skilled and committed professionals, not just law students, rely on contingency contracting to reinforce their preparation for critical performances in different fields.

Stages. Recognize that studies go through stages. Determine whether you need to start studying early. Whether or not you need an early start, set a start date for studying. Complete all significant administrative and management steps as early as you can so that they do not interfere with studies, whether having to do with registering for courses, taking time off from work, obtaining childcare, confirming your study location, ordering your course texts, or collecting study resources and supplies. Early preparation, even for just an hour or two a day, can familiarize you with materials while eliminating procrastination and relieving stress. Early in each term of law school, transition your studies from early preparation into routine effortful study. Remain attentive to your diet, exercise, and rest during this routine study period. Incorporate practice exams into your routine study even if an exam is not approaching so that your studies align to the assessment. If your course has interim tests, then expect intensive, comprehensive review and practice before each test. Expect the same before final examination. You should feel your studies gaining momentum through the term until you are expending maximum effort in intensive study. You should also have made all necessary and helpful adjustments by the time of the intensive stage.

Optimization. Recognize that one time can be worth more time than other time. Optimum study time is when you are fresh, energized, and focused, ready to perform. Down time is when you are weary, tired, and distracted. Identify your optimum time. Assess when you are feeling most fresh and focused, the times of day when you seem to accomplish the most. Your energy level and ability to concentrate and focus, together with the energy level and activities of those around you, will determine your optimum times. Once you identify those optimum times, *devote them to law studies.* Protect that time. Be jealous about that time. Draw lines around that time. Expend that time on law studies. Two hours of intense studies at your optimum time may be as productive as eight hours of low-energy, distracted studies. Rather than concentrating study into a single extended period, space study out over time. Breaking a subject up into smaller chunks for study spaced out over time helps move subjects from short-term to long-term memory. Cognitive studies also confirm the greater value of *interleaving* the study of related subjects one over the other, for moving learning from short-term to long-term memory. *Sequencing* one subject along with another subject may

71

slow your studies somewhat but can improve your recall of and testing on both subjects. Valuable retrieval and reorganization occurs each time you return to one subject from other subjects. When planning your schedule, space out and then also interleave, more so than block, your law studies.

Concentration. Take breaks for a few minutes each hour of your studies. Study for fifty minutes but then take a ten-minute break before beginning with the next hour of study. Move around on your breaks. Stretch, run up and down stairs, snack briefly, or brush your hair or teeth. Do *something* other than stare at a book or computer. Then return to your studies refreshed and ready to go for another forty-five to fifty minutes. You may have heard of runners using *interval training* to improve their stamina. As you approach exams, vary the length of your study sessions between shorter bursts of a half hour to an hour, and longer sessions of two to three hours. Although these sessions will tire you, you should nonetheless find your concentration and stamina growing stronger. The point is not to practice comfortably but instead to stretch your capacity. Concentration improves with rigorous practice.

Consistency. Whatever schedule that you plan, stick to it. You never get back the time that you lose. The race goes to the tortoise, not the hare. A little more each day adds up to much more than a lot jammed into a single day. Ten three- to four-hour days of law study mean much more than one or two twelve-hour or even sixteen-hour days. By keeping to your schedule, you are eliminating the need for catch-up, hurry-up, and makeup days that don't in any case produce the kind of effective learning that you need for success. When you do keep to your schedule, you gain a sense of accomplishment, assurance, and satisfaction that fuels you for sticking to your schedule the next day. Success breeds success. At the same time, when you fall off schedule, get up, brush yourself off, and get back on schedule. Expect to have unavoidable interruptions. Get past the interruption, don't beat yourself up unnecessarily, and then promptly return to schedule. Don't let falling off schedule keep you from trying to catch back up. And when you can't catch back up, don't let it bother you so badly that you give up sticking to the rest of the schedule. Be as consistent as possible.

Practice. While you may sense yourself going through phases beginning with grasping the basic law before you can begin to use it, do not delay in practicing test taking. You are far better off starting with practice tests a little too early than much too late. We learn better by doing than by simply hearing or seeing. Include in your schedule lots of time for practice tests, particularly where you get feedback that you can use to correct your answers and improve your written work. Don't worry if when taking early practice tests you are getting only half of the answers right. You should quickly begin to improve that early performance. Examinees regularly improve by five, ten, or even twenty percent from one practice test to another. Imagine instead if you had waited until late in preparations to take your first test but scored very poorly on it. Work plenty of practice into your schedule.

C. Resources

Acquire as early as you can the casebooks, texts, and other study aids that your law professor requires. The law school's bookstore will post online the resources that your law professor requires together with the first class's reading assignment. Do not wait until the first class to determine what books you need and what you need to read from them. Your professor will expect your knowledgeable participation in the first class. You may also be able to get the professor's syllabus online or directly from the professor before the first class. Beyond acquiring the resources that the professor requires, you have no need to feel that you are on your own in studying for a law degree. You have abundant other supporters and resources. When you gather advisors, tutors, mentors, review books, outlines, video and audio recordings, flashcards, and other resources around you, you draw on the insight and support of many who want you to succeed and have worked or will work hard to see you do so. Don't ignore the abundant study resources. Rather, explore those resources, including especially at your law school's library, choosing from among those resources what you need most at each stage of your studies. Your favorite initial resources may be review books and video and audio lectures. Yet you may soon be creating outlines and using flashcards, and before long answering practice questions with clear feedback. You may find particular instructors or study groups especially helpful at times but then may seek a former professor's clarification or end up drawing on a student mentor. Investigate potential resources as you discover them, and then choose, employ, and value the resources that mean the most to you at each stage of your preparation. Consider each of the following resources.

Outlines. Outlines, meaning concise summaries of the law usually in bullet-point format, are a significant tool when you prepare and use them properly. Making the perfect outline is not sufficient for law studies. You may know your outline inside and out but still not have the fluency to recall law or the skill to apply it. Because one part of the outline triggers the next part, you might be able to recall your whole outline but still not spot the important law issues in a fact pattern or analyze those facts using the law. Fact patterns, not outlines, must trigger law recall and application. Outlines are simply a way to ensure that you know law, not that you can recall and use it where you need to do. That said, developing a detailed, diagrammatic, one-page outline for each of your doctrinal law courses can be a very useful way of confirming and rehearsing your knowledge. Make your outline long enough to capture important detail but short enough to review repeatedly in its entirety including in the hour or two before examination.

Flashcards. You may wonder what advantage flashcards can have over a reliable outline. While the outline and flashcards should reflect the same substantive law, flashcards add several advantages. While one side of the flashcard states the same substantive law appearing in an outline, the card's reverse side carries only a brief trigger with which to associate that substantive law. The triggers could be single law terms or short law phrases, or they could be brief fact patterns or procedural context. By breaking down the concepts that you need to know into individual components on flashcards, and matching those components with pertinent triggers, you can more easily learn and recall those components while rehearsing troublesome terms or phrases. Flashcards also make it easier to precisely measure and assess your progress by counting the average number of cards you got right and wrong during timed trials. Watching your performance improve can motivate you while also providing feedback on the quality of your studies. Another advantage is that single cards isolate the law that you must recall from other information that might be serving as supportive context. Flashcards, shuffled and used in active, game-like fashion, can increase the speed, fluency, and accuracy of your recall on any law topic, in random order just as law exams and law practice tend to work. One of the most consistent findings from research on how people learn is that active practice is significantly more valuable than passive exposure. When you use flashcards correctly, they make learning an active experience. Consider adding flashcards as a helpful resource.

Recordings. Video recordings, supplied by your professor or available through other sources, are popular resources. You can watch video lectures at your leisure, skip or speed up parts that you already know, and repeat parts that you do not know. Quality and content can vary widely, some showing only the speaker while others show both the speaker and slide shows or other visual materials supporting the speaker's presentation, and still others showing only the visual materials without showing the speaker. An advantage of audio recordings over video recordings is that you can listen while driving, watching children, or doing housework, things that require your visual attention but not concentrated thought. Listening to an audio recording can repeat and reinforce learning, helping you move that learning from short-term to long-term memory. Use headphones or earbuds to listen to audio recordings while riding the bus, watching your children at the playground, or otherwise fitting in some study while out in public. Audio recordings can be a helpful supplemental resource. Do not, though, overestimate their value. Lulling yourself to sleep at night playing audio recordings of lectures is not studying. Indeed, unless you are simultaneously reviewing a programmed workbook or otherwise using a coordinated resource, audio recordings do not provide the visual stimuli and active engagement that would increase your uptake, understanding, organization, and recall. Audio recordings should not be your only resource.

Practice Questions. Law school involves periodic assessment. In some courses, you may draft documents or write papers that the professor will grade, while in skills courses you may negotiate, interview, counsel, mediate, advocate, or cross-examine. Foundational doctrinal courses, though, tend to have final exams if not also interim quizzes. Bar exams have similar written assessments. Quality practice questions are important study resources for law school and bar exams. Multiple-choice and essay questions, or other questions in the form with which your professor will test you, help you practice the actual performance rather than practice things that poorly approximate actual performance. Psychometrics experts at the National Conference of Bar Examiners share with law professors the Conference's guidelines for the sound design, form, and content of bar examination-like multiple-choice questions. You do best to practice questions of that standard, sound design rather than some other design. Ensure that you have quality practice questions available to you as a consistent resource. Ask your professor, academic advisor, law librarian, and student bar association for sound practice questions. Commercial bar-review courses, for which students often register early in law school, often provide abundant practice questions. Learn by practicing the performance.

Feedback. One of your greatest resources is feedback on practice multiple-choice and essay questions. You should not be simply practicing multiple-choice questions, looking at your score, and hoping to do better next time. Instead, you should be reviewing explanations both for your correct answers, because you may have guessed or used an incorrect rationale, and for your wrong answers to correct your answer and rationale. Practicing is alone not enough. You also need to evaluate your practice. You need to learn from both your correct and your wrong or incomplete answers. You can only do so when you are discerning the law, rule, or rationale that supports the correct and complete answer. You may be able to decipher that rationale using only the question and your outline or other substantive-law materials, but detailed answer explanations, model answers, and scoring rubrics can be better resources. Compare your answer to the model answer and scoring rubric. Get individual feedback on your practice essay answers from a rigorous reviewer such as your professor, an academic advisor, or a competent classmate. Ask a classmate to practice flashcards with you, helping you make active responses and ensuring that you measure progress.

Mentors. Deliberately seek out mentors as another resource. While you may feel the need to chart your own path, paths that others followed can give you clear clues about the direction most fitting for you. Do not overlook your law professors as mentors. They will have guided and supported hundreds of students, collecting in the course much wisdom. They may also know you well enough to give especially effective counsel. Find a family member, friend, or classmate to review your performance, confirm your goals, contact you periodically with encouragement, and be available for consultation. While you may also get law school advice from lawyers, be cautious in accepting advice from senior lawyers whose law school experience may have been very different from the one you will experience. Law school courses, curriculum, exams, resources, technology aids, learning theory, *and* the law have all changed a lot in the past decade or two and will continue to change.

D. Performances

By now, you should appreciate that to study effectively involves practicing the actual performance that the course, and eventually the bar exam and law practice, requires. One almost wishes that you could simply sit down for a law school exam to write out and reproduce your best course outline, except that the performance that law school exams and law practice require is clearly not reproducing class notes and outlines. Yet too many students prepare for exams as if reproducing outlines is all that success entails. They write and re-write outlines, and read and re-read outlines, without taking the next step of applying the law that those outlines summarize. Outlining law and memorizing outlines may be helpful because you need to know the law, but that form of study does not go far enough. Exams and law practice require *using* the law, not just recalling the law. You must practice the performance. At some point, and the earlier the better, you must get beyond your notes, summaries, and outlines. Practicing multiple-choice and essay questions early and often during your studies has you practicing the final course, and indeed also the bar-exam, performance. In your studies, concentrate on producing relevant *output*, particularly practice-exam answers, more so than amassing hours of input, like watching or listening to recordings, reading materials, and going over outlines. Treat law studies more like you would treat *working* than you would like traditional studying. The law firm that hires you will want your output, your performance on critical tasks, not simply your input, like logging hours in the law library. Not surprisingly, study of law students suggests that *work drive* correlates with academic success. Honestly, work (output, performance) satisfies much more than mere passive input.

Briefing. Case briefing is the first example of an important, even if only temporary, law-school performance or output. Law schools use orientation and academic-services programs to instruct law students in case briefing. Follow that instruction carefully, completing all case-briefing exercises in earnest. Learn to brief cases. Many first-year law professors require or strongly encourage case briefing. If the professor calls on you in class to recite about a case, but you have not briefed the case, then you stand a good chance of embarrassment in your recitation. Case briefing forces you to separate relevant from irrelevant facts, identify issues and rules that address them, discern case holdings, and articulate how the opinion justifies those holdings. These skills are fundamental to law practice. Lawyers use these skills every day. Many law students abandon case briefing after the first term or year because of the time and effort that it takes, they feel that they have have largely acquired the critical underlying skills, and they are practicing other performances such as drafting memoranda, agreements, and court papers, reviewing files, and of course practicing multiple-choice and essay questions. Do not skip the step of briefing cases early in law school, though. You need to acquire the fundamental skills of spotting issues, winnowing material from immaterial facts, discerning rules and holdings, and articulating case reasoning. Methods of case briefing vary. Follow the method in which your law school instructs.

Active Learning. If during your studies you find that you are holding too long and tightly to your notes and outlines without practicing the performance, then you may simply misunderstand how you learn. Studies show that the earlier one makes an effort to solve a problem, the better one learns the solution's criteria and procedures. Practicing problems before you have the knowledge can improve the speed and reliability at which you acquire that knowledge. Problems, whether essay or multiple-choice questions, or performance tests, help you create, correct, and confirm the logic constructs, schema, frameworks, and connections that aid recall. Some describe the difference as one between *passive learning* like reading, listening to audio tapes, and watching videos, and *active learning* like solving problems. Frequent active learning with feedback builds the law knowledge and skills you need. Practice problems, and then practice more problems, again and again, reviewing the answers and explanations even if you chose the correct answer. Rehearse the terms, concepts, and laws until you know them, then continue rehearsing until you know them fluently with your performance flowing smoothly. Be both accurate and quick with your knowledge. When you see law statements justifying an answer that you missed, read those law statements aloud, write them down, and rehearse them until you know the rule that led to the correct answer. Be as active in your law studies.

Timed Practice. Practice under the same time constraints that exams impose. You may initially practice using more time than an exam allows, as you confirm your knowledge, develop your skill, and improve the speed and fluency of your reading, thinking, recall, analysis, and writing. Soon, though, you should be practicing using the same time as the exam allows. You need to learn to read, recall, reflect, reason, and express your answer at the speed that the exam's time requires and at the level that the exam's time allows. Discerning every nuance of a multiple-choice question by mulling it over for far longer than the exam allows, or writing masterful, highly articulate, beautifully constructed essay answers using two or three times the period that the exam allows, will not help you develop the speed and fluency that you need for the exam. A large part of an exam's challenge, and a large part of its value, has to do with your fast and fluent recall and use of law knowledge. Deliberate reflective thought is not an option. You must learn to read, think, answer, and write so readily as to make your performance nearly automatic. The only way to do so is to practice within time constraints.

Quantity. How much study is enough study is an open question that may well vary from student to student. Even while we all need and benefit from study, some of us benefit from more study than do others of us. Yet the sheer quantity of study that some strong students have completed may surprise you and stimulate and challenge you to study more regularly and effectively. For example, successful bar examinees report answering 20, 30, or 50 multiple-choice questions every day for several weeks. They may practice periodic banks of 100 questions as bar-examination format requires. Bar-exam instructors may recommend completing at least 2,000 practice multiple-choice questions. That large of a quantity may be unusual but may also help you adjust your own objectives and increase your practice.

Successful examinees also report writing two to three essay answers every day while also reviewing those answers, accumulating into dozens or even hundreds of practice essay questions. Answering two to three practice essay questions each day would enable a bar examinee to practice all essay subjects with appreciable frequency.

Quality. The quality of your study, though, matters just as much as *or more than* the quantity. When you are practicing multiple-choice and essays questions, you should also be studying your answers. Review the explanations for your correct answers to multiple-choice questions to ensure that you know *why* you got the answer right. Review even closer the explanations for your incorrect answers to multiple-choice questions to ensure that you correct your law knowledge and improve your application skills. Watch for patterns in incorrect answers. If you are missing questions especially in a certain subject area, then focus your studies in that area while assessing the quality of your subject-area resource and making appropriate adjustments. Your materials or outlines on that subject may be inadequate or incorrect. Look for other patterns in your essay answers when comparing and contrasting them to model answers. If you frequently miss issues, then you may need to take additional time to read essay questions and outline essay answers. If you frequently miss rules, then you may need more practice on writing rule statements quickly and fluently. If you frequently skip analysis, then you may need more structure to your essay answers to ensure that you are applying law to each issue. Spend time analyzing your performance even while practicing your performance. Make your practice *quality* practice, not just quantity practice.

E. Behavior

Take a few moments to confirm the wisdom of the plans, programs, and practices advocated above, through the perspective of behavioral science. Succeeding in law school is behavior. Studying for exams is behavior. Practicing law is behavior. Your

81

ability to successfully manage your behavior underlies all of your personal and professional goals. Use behavioral science to bring out the best in your performance. Social scientists have studied learning extensively and in the process have established certain principles and debunked certain myths. Untrustworthy lore surrounds the subject of preparing for the law school exams. Some assertions accepted as truths are instead unhelpful, inaccurate, and misleading, frustrating rather than promoting your studies and performance. Use the following behavioral theory and evidence to evaluate the study advice that you hear while putting a check on the myths that you may start telling yourself as your studies proceed.

Motivation. First, understand your motivation and how motivation works. Sometimes we talk about motivation as purely an inner quality. Behavioral science shows instead that motivation can be any factor that pushes us toward goal-directed behavior, including external factors, not just inner reservoirs. To increase your motivation, alter those external factors. Law school can be intellectually arduous, even if it does not entail the physical effort, personal discomfort, and safety risk that other career-preparation programs like law enforcement, construction trades, and even medical school entail. Law school's steep intellectual challenge makes your motivation critical. You succeed largely because of the quantity and quality of your effort, not because you discover the kingdom's magic keys. Study success takes extended effort without shortcut. Do things to help yourself commit to that effort. Given that motivation is an important tool, recognize both your strongest motivators and strongest distractors. Given how desirable succeeding in law school is, that goal alone might well be sufficient to motivate you. Yet the truth may be that earning a law degree, passing the bar, and entering the law profession or a related field may be too distant as rewards to sufficiently affect motivation. Students strongly desire these and related positive outcomes, but behavioral science indicates that big future distant rewards often fail from day to day to motivate effectively.

Feelings. Part of the motivation problem is that your idle assessment of your progress, meaning how you *feel* that you are doing moment to moment and hour to hour, is highly unreliable, indeed often the opposite of your actual progress. Indeed, the better you feel from moment to moment, the less learning-boundary effort you may actually be putting forward. Students in any program sometimes forget this lesson, confusing ease with reward, when to the contrary learning is by nature not easy. The outcome of becoming a competent professional rewards, but the *process* of becoming competent does not *feel* rewarding, instead involving struggle to acquire necessary new knowledge and skills. The short-term experience of learning can feel confusing, clumsy, and awkward. You may feel exhausted after an hour of study, while your only immediate reward is a barely perceptible increase in your knowledge. Yet the only way to learn is through those small increases adding up. The point is not to judge by feelings.

Immediacy. Consider then how to solve the motivation problem that learning law presents. Our natural inclination is to avoid hard work that has only small immediate reward, even if that hard work would lead to large delayed reward. We have just seen that you need to work against your natural inclination because those small-but-cumulative gains are important in the long run. To do so, you need to contrive rewards and conditions that help push you past difficult but worthwhile obstacles. Graduating with a law degree, passing the bar exam, and entering law practice or a related field might seem like your strongest motivators, but better motivators in the short term are those that you arrange for frequent achievement. Create daily sources of motivation by collecting data on your performance so that you can see the incremental improvement in your skills. Find frequent sources of motivation by enlisting others to provide you with social consequences for daily achievements or shortcomings. Daily sources of motivation require planning and doing something that doesn't come naturally. Look for external sources of motivation that you can regularly arrange for yourself. Don't simply rely on some inner wellspring of motivation to carry you forward but also construct frequent small rewards.

Procrastination. Putting off until tomorrow what you can *and should* do today is your primary enemy in law studies, just as procrastination will be your enemy in your future law practice and is generally in life. A single big exam at the end of a course, on which your entire course result depends, is a poor design for motivation and excellent design for procrastination. Law school courses having only a single end-of-term assessment invite procrastination, when procrastination you cannot at all afford. This condition is part of the reason why an end-of-term exam may feel stressful. Rationally, an exam is no threat but instead simply tests a skillset that you could readily acquire by practicing those skills daily. Just distribute your practice and study over time, and you'll do fine. The problem is that we are not inherently rational creatures. We often do quite poorly particularly with small performances that are only important when they accumulate, and especially when that accumulation occurs over an extended period of time. Most of us could easily cite some self-improvement goal we failed to reach that required frequent effort for minimal daily improvement. Running goals, physical strength goals, and weight loss are good examples of goals that require consistent frequent effort producing only small weekly or even monthly improvements. Studying law falls firmly within the category of small-but-cumulative gains. Law studies provide little immediate noticeable benefit. Students thus often wait until they feel the pressure of an impending deadline, in other words *procrastinate*, before they start studying, leaving too little time to make the necessary cumulative gains.

Structure. Your prior education offset this natural tendency when your teachers provided the consequences for you. If you didn't study, then you would fail a quiz or suffer embarrassment in class in the very near future. Much of law school may lack this structure, leaving you to artificially build in due dates and consequences for yourself. An effective way to counteract the powerful single-terminal-test procrastination effect is to create and employ multiple staged quizzes leading up to the final test. Your challenge is in taking these staged quizzes seriously. If you continue to think that only the final exam counts, then you may not put your maximum effort into the staged practice quizzes or may not take them at all. Bargaining with yourself is all too easy, convincing yourself that you still have time to make up the difference. You may, in other words, succumb to procrastination under the influence of the single-terminal-test effect. To guard against this effect, set up multiple due dates and sub-goals in advance. Enlist the help of someone who won't tolerate you putting off your progress until tomorrow, just as many people hire fitness coaches to help them manage the small-but-cumulative gains associated with physical health. Find someone who will push you to meet, not delay, your sub-goals and cheer on rather than ignore or overlook your interim successes. If no one is available to help you in that way, then function as that person for yourself. *Do not bargain with yourself.* Putting that small amount of study time until tomorrow *will* hurt.

Cramming. Studies also show that practice distributed over time leads to better learning than cramming during mass practice sessions. Cramming for an exam creates high anxiety that interferes with learning. Delaying studies may result in discovering that you do not have enough time to adequately prepare. Instead, produce what behavioral scientists call the *repeated scallop effect* in which you put forward maximum effort multiple times leading up to the exam. Repeated maximum effort will only happen if you structure multiple due dates with consequences for both success and failure. What will you gain if you meet a sub-goal? What will you lose if you fail to meet a sub-goal? If the answer is to either question is *nothing*, then your study plan may fail. Small frequent rewards like a specialty coffee, music purchase, or massage can spur you on. Small frequent disciplines like extra practice or denial for a day of a favorite soft drink or television show can get you back on track. Remember that these sub-goals need to happen frequently. If the only consequences are to pass or not pass the exam, then you may end up procrastinating. Do not wait to experience consequences. Instead, motivate yourself daily. Each interim practice should spur you into repeated focused studies, the cumulative effect of which is high performance on the final exam. Beat the procrastination effect with multiple full-effort practices.

Distraction. Recognize that attractive distractions set themselves against that core motivator of improving your studies. Law school often offers attractive new liberties, particularly what to do with your study time. Strong temptations can exist to pursue gratifications in lieu of studying. Family members and friends may expect you to lighten up on your former seriousness and partake in the joys of your new liberty. Rest, recreation, relationships, travel, and pastimes may beckon. These competing activities may have a seize-the-moment allure to them. Social gatherings and entertainment opportunities may require you to participate right now or not at all. You may feel that you can delay studies another day. Family and friends may argue that you can simply study tomorrow, so you should spend time with them today. The problem is how easily and quickly those delays accumulate until it is too late to study in a reasonable manner.

Deferral. Recognize how these attractive opportunities distract you from and compete with your core motivation. Do not dismiss their power or effect. Instead, acknowledge their competition both to yourself and to others. Then deliberately set them aside to the extent necessary to improve your study habits and practice performances. Recognize openly and frequently that you are only delaying, not forgoing, those attractive opportunities. Let others know why you are temporarily sacrificing certain social activities. Ask others to help with your self-discipline rather than compete with it. Make public your sub-goals and progress so that others can understand and support you. Others may then become additional sources of support and motivation rather than distractions, especially when you explain your plan and rationale to them. Other opportunities for rest, recreation, relationships, travel, pastimes, and acquisitions, not to mention full-time highly compensated law-firm work, will be there for you after you earn

86

your law degree just as much and indeed more so than during your studies. You will also enjoy those pursuits more later than now, when you can give them greater guilt-free attention. You need not forego other gratifications entirely. Simply delay and defer some gratification until you can most enjoy it after having accomplished your study goals.

Other Motivation. You will find motivation in the intellectual stimulation of certain courses in law school, indeed to some degree all courses. Law fascinates. Moderate studies may, though, satisfy your intrinsic interest, when real academic success may well require more than moderate study. Quantity alone can make *study* an unpleasant word, even when the subjects entertain and fascinate. Instructor and peer approval can also be significant motivators in well-constructed seminars, as can approval from family and friends when you display law knowledge in social settings. Yet those after-the-fact motivators don't generally work either to motivate consistent in-depth studies. You need motivation now, not later. Acquiring useful new skills can motivate learners, but intense study effort leaves little time to use new skills. None of these other variables are powerful enough to ensure reliable motivation. Although big future goals inspired you to start this professional journey, those delayed rewards and even the interim satisfaction of new knowledge and skills are weak motivators for studying today. Instead, meeting your daily sub-goals and improving your practice performances, together with the attached small daily rewards and admonishments that you craft for motivation, will help you study more consistently and effectively. Smaller immediate rewards are the key to reliably motivating you to unlock your big future.

Monitoring. At the outset, learners generally underestimate the time that specific learning requires. We tend to think that learning will take less time than it does. Initially, you will leave too little time for assigned reading and other study, and either come to class or an exam unprepared or have to scramble and cram to perform as you desire. Monitor time and task. By tracking your own performance, you discover how much time and effort you need to invest for success. Watching improvements in your performance over time can also motivate you. Create a visual graph of your practice performances over time. Observe the direction of your performance until you can see how each small gain steadily contributes to a larger overall improvement, making those small gains more meaningful. Watching your own performance inch closer and closer to your goals can be exciting. Behavior that we measure tends to matter the most to us. Frequent feedback is a source for both assessment and motivation. If instead you wait for the final exam, without frequent practice exams, then you may well find yourself either unprepared or cramming. You will only have a single piece of feedback in the form of a final grade, leading inevitably to procrastination. Instead, monitor, assess, and improve.

Myths. One myth prevalent among learners even in graduate and professional education is that quality instruction and resources are sufficient to motivate and produce adequate performance. The thought is that if you just sign up for the right course with the right professor, find the right outline, and work with the right study partner, then you will prepare adequately for the final exam. Yet effective performance is too subtle for inputs to work without rigorous assessment. You instead need frequent practice exams and other practice performances along the way, together with frequent consequences. A second myth is that scores on practice exams don't matter because you can readily ramp up performance for a real exam. To the contrary, a real exam may have just as many distractors as, or more distractors than, practice exams. If you do not perform well on practice exams, then you won't perform well on real exams. A final myth is that concentrating when attending lectures, watching videos, listening to audio recordings, and reading materials determines the quality of your performance. To the contrary, you do not know the quality of your performance *until you measure it*, either in practice or real performances. Don't accept the myths. Go with the behavioral science and facts.

> **Study.** Rate yourself from 1 for poor to 5 for excellent on each of the above sections as to your effectiveness at (1) deploying learning strategies, (2) sticking to study schedules, (3) locating reliable resources, (4) engaging in productive practice, and (5) managing your behaviors to best effect.

IX. What Is Law Practice?

A. Law Profession

Practitioners. Now, let's turn our attention to the practice of law, as another way to help you build your commitment to preparing for becoming a lawyer. Think first about the practitioners who comprise the justice system. Lawyers, judges, prosecutors, public defenders, corrections and probation officers, regulators, and others who operate the justice system are in one sense the law. Law is largely what the professionals who interpret and enforce law believe law to be. Law's sources, structures, and systems shape and define law. The ways in which lawyers organize for law practice also has a lot to do with the nature, quality, and effectiveness of the justice system, when the justice system is immensely important to individual Americans and to the American people as a whole. Consider then the following outline of the law profession.

Legal Education. Law schools became common in the early 20th century, largely replacing apprenticeship by the latter half of the 20th century. The law profession still controls legal education. The U.S. Department of Education authorizes a council of the American Bar Association, the largest national private professional organization of lawyers (indeed of any kind), to accredit law schools. Although much of law is state law, and state laws vary, law schools tend teach a national view of state law rather than solely teaching the law of specific states. Law-school faculties control curriculum content, guided by accreditation standards and accountable to students, employers, and bar examiners. Foundational courses tend to include the laws of care (tort law), covenant (contract law), restraint (criminal law), consent (constitutional law), and prosperity (property law) on which any society depends. Skills courses include the writing, ethics, and clinical instruction accreditation standards require. Law-school curricula may also focus on preparing students for bar-tested subjects like family law and sales or practical subjects like estate planning, tax practice, and business planning. The curriculum also allows students to explore specialty concentrations like intellectual property, administrative law, environmental law, international law, health law, labor law, corporate finance, real-estate transactions, and advanced litigation practice.

Law Instruction. Socratic examination remains law school's signature method. Law professors teaching doctrinal studies may challenge students to articulate the reasoning on which appellate courts have decided certain cases, sharpening students' ability to think analytically and evaluate rationales. Law schools have more recently learned to help students integrate doctrinal knowledge into a more balanced, whole, positive, and useful professional identity. Law schools do so through course offerings and co- and extra-curricular activities that may include portfolios, journals, competitions, clinics, student organizations, volunteer and pro-bono activities, internships and externships, seminars, and directed study. Law school is not solely about what goes on in the classroom or a transcript reflects. These integrative activities serve, together with post-graduate law-firm and judicial clerkships, as a transition into law practice.

Licensure. State laws require a license to practice law. Depending on the state, practicing law without a license may be a crime punishable by fine or imprisonment. State bar associations license lawyers, controlling admission to law practice. Lawyers admitted to the bar become officers of the court, meaning that they assume public duties and receive public powers to help administer justice. State bars generally require that an applicant for admission hold a degree from an accredited law school or an in-state law school recognized by the state supreme court. State bars also require examination for licensure. Nearly all state bars require applicants to pass the Multi-State Bar Exam and Multi-State Professional Responsibility Exam, while many also require passage of other testing focusing on the state's specific laws. State bars also require applicants to demonstrate good character and fitness.

Student Practice. Law students have opportunities to work in law firms, courts, agencies, and clinics under the supervision of licensed lawyers. Law students often serve as law clerks within law firms and courts, doing legal work not directly for clients but instead for lawyers and judges. Law firms treat law clerks differently than legal assistants. Legal assistant is a career role, not generally treated as a step toward legal education, a law degree, and law practice. Legal assistants may do much of the same work as law clerks but also perform additional clerical and administrative work. Law students have other opportunities beyond clerking. Many states approve law students for limited law practice within a law-school clinic or externship program supervised by a lawyer. You may have a meaningful opportunity to practice law during your legal education.

Lawyer Conduct. State bars, supreme courts, or their designated commissions and boards regulate the practice of licensed lawyers. Most states adopt some form of the ABA Model Rules of Professional Conduct. Lawyer conduct rules require diligence, honesty, candor, competence, character and fitness, loyalty, confidentiality, avoidance of conflicts, and other attributes and behaviors critical to public trust in the administration of justice. Anyone may complain of lawyer misconduct to state grievance officials who can impose lawyer discipline from reprimand to license suspension or revocation, for rules violations.

Legal Services. Lawyers play critical roles in politics and governance, administration and regulation, business formation and management, community support and development, dispute resolution, and preserving and promoting individual rights and liberties. Lawyers constituted more than half of the Constitution's

signers.   English orator Sir Edmund Burke celebrated the
emerging American nation as having the greatest law knowledge
among its citizenry while crediting that knowledge for the
population's general resourcefulness. More than half of American
presidents have been lawyers. The work of lawyers was critical to
averting   worldwide   financial   collapse   in   2008.   American
businesses depend on lawyers to protect and promote innovation
and   new   technologies.   Lawyers   enforce   state   and   local
ordinances, and help individuals and businesses work with state
and local officials, to promote order and security in local
commerce and communities.   Lawyers help individuals and
families with the transfer of wealth between generations and in
crises over divorce, child custody and support, job loss, housing
issues, financial and insurance disputes, and accidental death and
serious injury.

Service Delivery. Lawyers provide these critical law services
through direct employment by government or government-
funded agencies, in corporate-counsel offices of businesses, and in
large and small law firms or solo practice. Government employs
lawyers as judges, magistrates, trustees, clerks, and prosecutors,
in public defender offices, in planning and regulatory roles, and as
agency chiefs, managers, and advisors.   For-profit corporations
employ lawyers in executive, financial, human-resource, and
other administrative roles, and for risk management, litigation
management, negotiation, and other dispute resolution, and for
planning,   ethics,   and   regulatory   compliance.   Nonprofit
organizations employ lawyers as executive directors and in other
management and advisory roles. Large law firms having as many
as 100, 500, or even 1,000 lawyers provide similar services to
government and businesses.   More than half of all lawyers in
private practice work alone or in small firms of ten or fewer
lawyers, providing direct law services to individuals, families,
and small businesses. Private delivery of law services represents
the distinctly American culture of private property, rights, and
responsibility.

Financing Services. Insurance plans for pre-paid legal services are the exception rather than the rule. Indigent defendants charged with crimes likely to lead to incarceration have a constitutional right to free legal representation. Public defender's offices staffed with employee lawyers may provide that representation, or private lawyers in solo practice or smaller firms may provide those services either by contract with the local government or individual appointment from assigned-counsel lists maintained by local courts. Lawyers provide the vast majority of law services, though, through individual retainer agreements with individual paying clients. Lawyers provide services on hourly fees charged to clients in monthly bills for specific matters, or at flat rates for standardized services such as wills, trusts, powers of attorney, and forming a new business. Hourly and flat rates depend on the lawyer's skill, experience, and reputation, the client's ability to pay, and the market for law services in the geographic area and specialty field. In personal-injury, wrongful-death, worker's compensation, and Social Security disability cases, lawyers often work on contingency fees in which they receive a percentage of the client's recovery if any. Contingency fees make law services available to those who cannot afford them. In the American system, parties pay their own lawyer's fees in most cases.

Need for Services. Despite public and private delivery mechanisms for law services, studies suggest that lawyers do not satisfy all service needs. Federal, state, and local government supplement the private market for law services with publicly funded legal-aid organizations and legal assistance centers. Some lawyers pursue careers with legal-aid clinics, helping tenants in disputes with property owners, families in need of public services and benefits, victims of domestic violence, and other indigent and low-income clients. Litigants without a lawyer can increasingly find assistance with legal forms and information through court-based centers supported by public funding and private contributions and staffed by lawyers, legal assistants, law students, and other volunteers. Lawyers may also provide free legal representation through pro-bono programs. Lawyers who perform pro-bono service not only increase access to and the credibility of the justice system, provide critical private help and needed public service, and improve the image of the profession. They also improve their skills, expand their knowledge of new practice areas, broaden and deepen their network of client and professional relationships, and increase their standing and reputation within the bar and community.

Law Firms. Traditionally, law firms employ lawyers in a two-tier hierarchy of partners and associates. Conduct rules discourage lawyers from simultaneously offering brokerage, accounting, insurance, and other non-law services, and prohibit non-lawyer ownership of law firms. As a result, most lawyers work alone or with other lawyers in law firms providing only law services. Law firms generally hire new lawyers into associate rather than partner positions, giving associates several years to build their own client base while earning a partnership offer. Firms pay associates salaries at levels that enable the firm's partners to profit from the work of associates for clients with whom the partners maintain the relationship. Associate success in making partner often depends on the associate's ability to build a client base of the associate's own or to maintain strong client relationships. Associates who do not receive a partnership offer usually leave the firm to join another firm or for solo practice, government service, or other professional opportunity. No matter the organization, though, the economic success of a lawyer providing direct law service to individuals or businesses tends to depend on the lawyer's ability to attract and competently serve clients.

Judges. Judges in the United States have the same education and training as, and come from the ranks of, lawyers. Law-school graduates do not move directly into judicial positions. Those positions require several years of licensure and the prominence, skills, and reputation of an experienced lawyer. Law-school graduates seeking judicial positions may clerk for a judge, become active in state and local bar associations, develop litigation skills and experience, and nurture the contacts and reputation that will win judicial appointment or election. The president appoints federal judges on the U.S. Senate's advice and consent, to serve for a life term. Federal magistrate and administrative judges serve for limited terms. State governors appoint judges in many states while other states elect judges. Elected judges usually have the advantage of running on ballots that designate them as incumbents, with electorates very likely to retain incumbents. Elected judges may retire shortly before the next election in order to allow a governor having the same party affiliation to appoint a replacement who then runs as an incumbent, making many elected judgeships effectively controlled by appointment. Judges are more than arbiters of important legal issues. They are also symbols of the law, robed and elevated to reflect the elevated status we accord law. Judges, like lawyers, must conform to conduct rules enforced by judicial tenure commissions that remove judges who harass parties or staff, accept bribes, or otherwise abuse judicial powers.

Women in the Profession. American law schools began to enroll significant numbers of women and members of racial minorities only in the 1970s. Harvard Law School barred women until 1950. Washington and Lee Law School barred women until 1972. Until 1971, women lawyers represented 3% or less of the profession. By 1980, women were 34% of J.D. candidates and 8% of the profession. By 2000, women were 27% of the profession and approaching 50% of J.D. candidates. The entry of women into the profession has influenced the law in many areas including pregnancy and disability rights, domestic-violence prevention, and workplace sexual harassment while also influencing law practice in areas like pregnancy and parental-care leave, flexible and part-time schedules, telecommuting and contract services, and alternative careers.

Inclusion. Until the 1980s, most African-American lawyers had attended one of the nation's four predominantly black law schools. Minority J.D.-candidate enrollment increased from 5,568 in 1971 to 29,489 in 2004, the latter representing 21% of J.D.

candidates. African-American lawyers increased from 1% of the profession in 1970 to 4.2% in 2000, by which time minority lawyers constituted 12.9% of the profession. Despite advances, African Americans remain significantly underrepresented in the profession when compared to the general population, as do Hispanics and Latinos, Native Americans, and Asian Americans. Minority underrepresentation is particularly acute at higher levels within the profession, where in 2000 minority lawyers still comprised only 3.3% of law-firm partners. A 2005 American Bar Association report reflected that while only 9.7% of lawyers in the United States are ethnic minorities, minorities comprise 20.8% of accountants, 24.6% of physicians, and 18.2% of college professors. Just as it did in the case of women, the presence of increasing numbers of minority lawyers has influenced the law and its practice in a variety of ways through committed and effective leadership, service, and scholarship. All lawyers share the responsibility to ensure equal access to the law profession.

Study. Suppose an acquaintance commits her law career to reform the child-welfare system in her metropolitan area, after the latest tragedy over child abuse and neglect. What employment or practice structure would you recommend to her to best achieve her career goal?

B. Law's Sources

Law's Theory. Just as you must know the law profession to succeed in law school, you must also know the nature and sources of law. In its utilitarian sense, law involves coercive enforcement of formally recognized social norms, for the good of the greatest number. Laws are state-sanctioned rules of conduct applying generally to society's members. We each relinquish some individual liberty to ensure relatively equal degrees of liberty for all. Law defines those out-of-bounds activities against which the state lends force in order to prohibit. Yet beyond its utilitarian purpose, law justifies itself in the duty it imposes, virtue it promotes, and sanctity it preserves for individuals within society. Just look at us. We are inherently purposeful, constantly having ends in mind. But we are also conscious of the purposes of others. And so there arises in the crucible between our purposes and the purposes of others a necessity to respect one another. The Judeo-Christian expression is to love one another as ourselves. Its Kantian expression is the categorical imperative to treat others as ends rather than means, such that all could accept our every action as a general rule.

Law's Limits. The behavior law requires or prohibits is narrower than the behavior morals and ethics require or prohibit. Morals shine in darkness only the depths of which law regulates. Given our propensity for mischief, any society that attempted to restrict every deleterious behavior would have nothing to do other than administer law. Law must instead direct itself to actions that affect the life, liberty, and property of others. Yet the quality of thought behind action, such as whether it was malicious, reckless, or careless, can determine legal outcomes. Law does not concern itself solely with results. Law instead reflects the history, experience, and wisdom of a people. Archaeologists find law written on the earliest fragments of cuneiform text. Hammurabi used a law code to administer an empire nearly 2,000 years before the great Roman codes. Moses reconstituted Israel as a nation around the Ten Commandments. While law has its limits, law nonetheless has broad purposes and influence.

Natural Law. Law's modern history began in earnest in the 17th century with European natural-law scholar Samuel Pufendorf whom scholars credit as the first secular university law professor. Natural law, which the Declaration of Independence calls "the Laws of Nature and of Nature's God," is a deductive system fitting law to the natural character and conditions of those whom it governs. Natural-law concepts of justice, proportion, equality, equity, responsibility, compassion, and fairness continue to underpin and inform modern law. England's great 18th-century law chronicler William Blackstone, United States Supreme Court Justice Joseph Story who lent credibility to Harvard's new Law School, great 19th-century American treatise-writers like Chancellor Kent and Justice Cooley, and civil-rights leader Martin Luther King Jr. all thought and wrote within natural-law traditions. Natural law concerns itself with individual rights and duties, the quality of individual decisions and acts measured against the experience of human nature, and preserving right relationship to the eternal and among persons, as the most-reliable source of human flourishing.

Other Schools. While lawyers, judges, and jurors continue to employ natural-law concepts, other theoretical schools dominate law scholarship. Legal-realist and historical schools hold that law is not inherent in nature but instead the product of peculiar cultural, social, and economic views of judges. Legal realism and historicism diminish law's moral and normative content, treating law more so as power in a Darwinist stance that society progresses through historical epochs and social developments in a survival of the fittest. The legal-process school discerns structural and procedural constraints on legal realism's raw power. Legal positivism treats law less as what it should be than what it is, looking to the enactments of legislatures and statements of judges. Critical legal theorists hold that law has no principled structure, instead inculcating the biases and preserving the advantages of the dominant class. Economic and sociological analyses of law use the concepts and methods of those disciplines to explain, justify, and shape law. Legal pragmatism considers the laws that officials can adopt and enforce effectively within their means and resources. Postmodernist, feminist, communitarian, and civic-republican schools also influence law in a healthy American melting pot of commitments and interests.

Constitutions. Fundamentally, though, the source of American law lies in the various state constitutions that create state executives, legislatures, and courts, and in the federal Constitution creating a national executive, legislature, and judiciary. The states adopted the U.S. Constitution in 1789 and

100

have amended it rarely since. States frequently adopt and amend new state constitutions. The state and federal constitutions do not contain much law within their own texts. Reproducing the entire text of the U.S. Constitution and all 50 state constitutions requires but a few hundred pages. The U.S. Constitution is the people's grant of limited federal-government powers, reserving all other powers to the states as they provide in their own state constitutions. Given limited federal powers, most of property law, contract law, tort law, criminal law, family law, and other laws affecting daily life are state, not federal.

Common Law. American law has its roots in England's common-law system. The common law is a body of legal rules and precedents that lawyers and judges draw from decided cases. England gradually developed both a common-law jury system and equitable remedies administered without juries. The distinction between law and equity remains important today in determining whether a party has the right to a jury trial. In a common-law system, every judge's decision has its own authority for the decided case while also adding to the common law's decisions, traditions, and customs. Because lawyers draw the common law from many cases rather than a single legislative code, common-law systems are essentially practitioner rather than expert systems. The common law fits historical American commitments respecting individual conscience and liberty, while mistrusting professional classes and authoritarian elites and edicts. Your lawyer can be as important as the law.

Controlling Authority. Lawyers and judges rely first on cases that they find within their own judicial system. A lawyer who has a state claim to maintain or defend will look first to the cases decided in that state, if the state has any, and only then to other states' cases. A lawyer who has a matter involving federal law will look to federal cases beginning with Supreme Court decisions and then to cases in the local federal circuit and district, before looking if necessary to other circuits and districts. Appellate courts tend to follow their own prior decisions (decisions by the same court, even though its judges or justices will change over time) on like cases, for fairness, predictability, efficiency, and credibility. Higher courts bind lower courts in the same system. Thus case precedent works both horizontally within the same court over time and vertically from the superior to the inferior courts. Appellate courts tend to overrule their prior decisions and change the common law only when society changes to the point that the prior rule has become unworkably inefficient, no longer reflects social policy or conscience, or is otherwise clearly erroneous.

Applying Authority. Your first year of law school will stress that you develop strong analytical skills. You will learn deductive systems of identifying claims and charges, recalling their elements, and applying them to settled facts to arrive at and justify decisions. Yet the common law does not act deductively. It is primarily an inductive system, meaning that lawyers and judges treat the peculiar facts and circumstances of each case as primary, deriving principles of law from those facts. Courts make common law by deciding individual cases, each of them different in detail even if often falling into patterns with other similar cases. The power of the common law is analogical as much as analytical. You must decide your new case consistent with similar circumstances reflected in old cases that you have located and read. The process of comparing and contrasting facts tends to reveal the nature, scope, and basis for the legal rule on which to decide the new case. Case precedent increases fairness, predictability, efficiency, and legitimacy of the legal system. Do not be unduly concerned over your ability to reason analogically. Analogy is a natural form of thinking and learning.

Statutory Law. Despite American law's common-law nature, statutory law remains vastly important to the administration of justice in the United States. Congress and the state legislatures adopt specific statutory provisions in a host of specific instances affecting the common law of torts, contracts, property, crimes, and other areas. Services compile these legislative acts into federal and state codes that lawyers use to research statutory provisions. When a statute applies and its language is clear and controlling, courts typically rely on the statute, not on case law. Statutory law, where it exists, is usually supreme over case law. Yet even in those cases, lawyers and judges will often rely on cases showing when and how courts properly apply the statute. The necessity for courts to construe statutes in any specific instance and gaps national and state legislatures leave by not writing comprehensive laws leaves substantial room for the common law to flourish.

Administrative Law. Federal and state administrative agencies promulgate rules and regulations significantly affecting individual rights and responsibilities. Most agencies are units of the executive branch of federal or state government, while some are independent. Legislation creates agencies, which must act consistent with their authorizing statutes. Agencies carry out their legislative mandates in part by promulgating rules and regulations. Agency rule-making power can substantially affect individual life, liberty, and property. Procedure acts therefore require agencies to publish proposed rules, permit public comment on proposed rules, discuss and respond to public comments, modify proposed rules on the basis of public comments, and otherwise demonstrate that the agencies have acted in a reasoned manner. The procedures acts allow individuals and entities to challenge in court those agency actions that violate mandated rule-making procedures. Administrative law judges hear and decide administrative claims for Social Security and worker's compensation benefits, labor rights, licenses to conduct regulated businesses or participate in regulated professions, and other matters. Many lawyers practice solely or primarily in administrative-law contexts.

Legal Research. When state supreme courts and mid-level appellate courts decide cases, they often write opinions citing statutes, case law, rules, and regulations, while explaining their application. Legal-research services collect and publish case opinions in reporter systems. In the federal system, reporters publish U.S. Supreme Court, Circuit Court of Appeals, and District Court decisions. Lawyers and judges research and rely on published decisions when evaluating, advocating, and deciding cases. Lawyers today use electronic databases to search for decisions of specific courts or groups of courts on certain fact and law issues. Lawyers also use electronic and print annotations, head-note systems, and digests to locate applicable decisions and confirm that the laws the decisions reflect remain current. Statutory research proceeds similarly. Lawyers also use e-journal, listserv, treatise updates, weekly and monthly periodicals, newsletters, seminars, and conferences to stay current on the law in their field. Student law reviews publish scholarly articles. Lawyers also read practical writings published by national, state, and regional bars, bar specialty sections, and continuing legal education institutes.

Study. You represent an industry association whose officers have asked that you write a friend-of-the-court brief supporting a Supreme Court challenge to the constitutionality of a burdensome industry regulation. What sources of law are you likely to research and cite for your brief?

C. Law's Structure

Federalism. You cannot understand American law without recognizing its basis in federalism. Thirteen previously sovereign American colonies formed the federal government by consent. The states are not divisions of a single national government. They instead retain aspects of consenting sovereigns. The colonies did not relinquish sovereignty with the 1776 Declaration of Independence, nor with the 1781 Articles of Confederation. The states did relinquish critical aspects of sovereignty including treaty-making powers, national defense, monetary policy, and interstate commerce, with the 1787 Constitution taking effect in 1789. The Constitution created a national legislature Congress with limited rather than general law-making powers. Dividing power between federal and state sovereigns checks and balances government and political power while ensuring more voices in democratic processes. Where state and federal law conflict, federal law controls. The supremacy clause of the federal Constitution expressly provides that the Constitution and all federal laws and treaties bind the states.

State Power. Under the Constitution's 10th Amendment, the states retain the powers that they did not expressly grant to the federal government through the Constitution. State power includes general law-making such as to provide for criminal law, family law, property law, tort law, and contract law. States organize government authority in a similar fashion as the federal government. The citizens of a state adopt a state constitution providing for the structure and authority of state government. State constitutions are supreme over state statutes and administrative regulations. Local government exercises similar legislative authority through ordinance (the local equivalent of statutes) and administrative regulation. State legislatures authorize local government, meaning that local governments are not sovereign.

Separation of Powers. Just as federalism defines American law, so too does the principle of separation of powers among branches of government. The U.S. Constitution divides federal power among legislative, executive, and judicial branches. In theory, the legislature makes law, the executive enforces law, and the judiciary applies and interprets law. In practice, though, each branch includes some degree of law-making, law-enforcement, and law-interpretation powers. As with federalism, the Constitution's drafters intended separation of powers to create additional checks and balances against the ability of any one branch, party, ideology, or faction to acquire so much power as to exercise it to the detriment of others' rights and interests. The three branches of government holding different powers depend heavily on one another to accomplish the ends of government. State constitutions structure state government similarly for similar reasons, mimicking the federal Constitution in forming legislative, executive, and judicial state branches.

Legislative Branch. Congress, comprised of the Senate and House of Representatives, holds the Constitution's Article I legislative powers. Those powers include to tax, provide for defense and general welfare, grant credit, regulate commerce among the states and with tribes and nations, coin and regulate money, and make all laws necessary and proper for carrying out those enumerated powers. The interstate-commerce clause and supporting necessary-and-proper clause together offer Congress its broadest powers. The Supreme Court interprets Congress' commerce powers broadly, meaning that we have a stronger rather than weaker federal government. State constitutions similarly vest legislative power in bicameral state legislatures except in Nebraska, which has a unicameral (one-body) legislature.

Executive. The President holds the Constitution's Article II executive powers. Those powers include to execute the laws adopted by Congress, act as commander in chief over military forces, appoint executive officers, enter into treaties with the Senate's advice and consent, and administer federal law through executive agencies and regulations. The President's power to create and direct administrative agencies gives the federal government its broadest reach. Congress enacts legislation authorizing administrative regulation and funding administrative agencies directed by the Executive Branch. The executive branch employs vast numbers to carry out its ends, far more than the other two branches. State constitutions form state executive branches led by governors, with state legislatures authorizing state executive agencies.

Judicial. The Constitution's Article III vests the federal government's judicial power in the U.S. Supreme Court. The Supreme Court decides cases between states while also ensuring reasonably uniform interpretation of federal law. The Supreme Court also maintains the constitutional order among branches of the federal government, between federal and state government, and between government and individual. The federal supremacy clause, federal Bill of Rights, and principles of federalism and separation of powers require the federal judiciary to decide many major issues affecting American law. The Supreme Court confirmed that power in 1803 in *Marbury v. Madison* when it declared the judiciary's power to review the constitutionality of statutes. Article III permits Congress to establish additional federal courts. Congress did so in 1789, creating a federal judiciary to decide federal questions and cases involving citizens of different states in trial-level United States District Courts in each state, from which parties can appeal to United States Courts of Appeal in 11 circuits plus the District of Columbia. The Supreme Court exercises discretion to take a limited number of appeals from the Circuit Courts.

State Courts. State constitutions and statutes create similar state judicial branches comprised of state supreme courts, mid-level appellate courts (in many though not all states), and trial courts. As much attention as law schools give to federal court decisions, the state courts, having general rather than limited jurisdiction, hear far more cases. Litigants file more than 30 million cases in state courts every year compared to about 300,000 new cases each year in federal courts. Only 1 out of about every 100 new lawsuits are in federal rather than state court. The states employ about 30,000 judges contrasted with the 1,500 federal judges, making for a ratio of about 20 to 1 in state to federal judges. State-court judges handle about five times as many cases as federal-court judges. The large number of cases in state court together with limited state resources distinguish state from federal litigation practice.

Individual Rights. State and federal constitutions play another significant role in American law by protecting individual rights. The U.S. Constitution's first ten amendments comprise the Bill of Rights guaranteeing the free exercise of religion, freedom from government-established religion, free speech and press, freedom of assembly, the right to bear arms, freedom from unreasonable government search and seizure, a privilege against self-incrimination, the right to confront witnesses in a criminal proceeding, due process and equal protection of law, and several other important rights. State constitutions provide similar or more-expansive rights. The U.S. Supreme Court has declared other rights implied within these express rights, such as a right to privacy over birth control and abortion. Federal and state constitutional guarantees protect against government action, not actions by private individuals. Federal and state statutes and the common law protect private individuals and entities from one another in ways different from these constitutional guarantees.

Due Process. Following the Civil War, the states amended the U.S. Constitution with the 13th Amendment abolishing slavery, the 14th Amendment prohibiting states from depriving persons of due process and equal protection of law, and the 15th Amendment prohibiting states from denying rights based on race, color, or prior servitude. The U.S. Supreme Court has interpreted the 14th Amendment's due-process clause to greatly expand the reach of the Bill of Rights to protect persons against not merely federal but also state authority when it interferes with federal constitutional and statutory rights.

Substance and Procedure. Law addresses matters of both substance and procedure. Substantively, law prohibits certain conduct, authorizing sanctions and remedies for law violations. Law's substance represents shared understandings of how we best preserve and promote human flourishing. Yet a justice system that had nothing but substantive rules for conduct would be ineffective or chaotic in its implementation. Law must also provide procedural rules through which to determine law violations. Procedures distribute and balance power among disputants consistent with the constitutional guarantee of due process or, as the Magna Carta first invoked it, the *law of the land* or rule of law. We govern one another only under substance and procedure that equate with fundamental rights and fundamental fairness. Due process means notice and opportunity for hearing whenever life, liberty, or property is in dispute in a government-supported proceeding.

Law's Authority. Instances arise in which it is not immediately clear which law applies, whether that of one state or another state, or of the federal law of the United States or some other country, especially when those laws differ or conflict. Choice of law and conflicts of law raise questions of when a state or nation should allow its courts to hear matters involving interstate or international matters, which state's or nation's law the courts should apply in those cases, and under what conditions to give effect to adjudications that other states or nations make. These questions can arise in interstate cases involving parties with interests in different American states, cases in American federal or state courts involving international affairs, and cases adjudicated in the courts of foreign nations. A court must also have authority over both the subject matter of the dispute and the parties involved in it.

Study. You represent a small-business owner on whom state regulators just served an OSHA citation indicating that the regulators may fine the business thousands of dollars and potentially close the business. Explain to your small-business-owner client the structure of state and federal branches of government within which officials issued and will resolve the citation.

D. Law's Systems

Civil Justice. Federal and state courts in the United States support both a civil-justice and criminal-justice system. Civil litigation is a state-sanctioned means of bringing private disputes to peaceful conclusions. The world regards Americans as unduly litigious, but the prominence of civil litigation in the United States represents our preference to resolve important issues by private interaction rather than through government administration. We trust our ability to adjust interests among ourselves more than we trust bureaucracies to adjust those interests for us. Civil litigation is necessarily adversarial. Courts do not create cases. Individual parties bring disputes to them. The civil-justice system is an immensely powerful and relatively efficient way of adjusting interests without oppressive government involvement. When parties do initiate litigation, more than nine out of ten cases resolve before trial. This private dispute-resolution system reduces the cost of administering public law across our vast continent while respecting Americans' historical distrust for distant governance.

Jury Trial. The right to a jury trial in many disputes fundamentally defines the American justice system. Juries keep the justice system accountable to local interests while promoting public trust and involvement in governance. The fact that American justice relies on juries has several practical consequences. Once a court constitutes a jury, the jury must decide the matter relatively promptly. A court cannot readily hold a jury to deciding a dispute over the course of months or years. Jurors move, fall ill, forget, die, and are subject to influence. The justice system also does not compensate jurors at a rate commensurate with ordinary employment. Jurors earn a relative pittance. Courts must therefore concentrate disputes into orderly, expeditious, continuous, and relatively short-term trials.

Pleading. If disputing parties have only a single relatively brief trial, then court rules must require parties to plead the claims and defenses defining clearly the trial's scope and the matters the trial is resolving. Pleading begins with the plaintiff filing a court complaint. The court then issues a summons requiring the defendant to defend the action. If the defendant has immediate grounds to dismiss the action, then the defendant may file a motion with the court asking for dismissal and a brief arguing its grounds. The court will hear the lawyers for the parties argue the motion in court and then rule from the bench at the hearing or write a decision. Trial judges dismiss a significant percentage of cases at these early stages of litigation for lack of legal merit.

Pretrial. For cases that move beyond the pleading stage, fairness requires that the parties discover the other side's evidence so as not to suffer prejudice by surprise at trial. Parties typically engage in discovery of the other side's evidence through document requests, written interrogatories, and depositions. Pretrial discovery motions, motions to amend pleadings to add parties and claims, and motions for summary judgment on undisputed facts are common. Courts issue pretrial orders and hold pretrial conferences to regulate these pretrial proceedings. Pretrial orders require the parties to file witness and exhibit lists to ensure a fair trial. Pretrial orders may also address admitted and disputed facts, applicable law, and prohibited arguments and evidence. Civil litigation can entail extensive discovery and pretrial procedures, allowing parties to prepare for their one opportunity at just resolution.

Jury Trial. Jurors typically have no legal training or experience with litigation. Jury trials therefore rely on rules of evidence to ensure that jurors hear only relevant evidence in a manner in which they will give that evidence its proper weight. Judges ensure an order and presentation of proofs that will not mislead jurors. Judges also instruct jurors on burdens of proof to ensure that jurors understand which party must present how much evidence to prove what elements of which claims. Jury trials also often involve not just lay witnesses but also expert witnesses who opine on special matters beyond the jurors' knowledge and experience. These and other features related to jury trials give American litigation a complexity not found in other justice systems. Cases tried to the bench, meaning decided by a judge acting without a jury, follow similar but sometimes abbreviated trial procedures.

Order of Trial. Jury trials typically begin with a random draw of jurors followed by lawyer questioning to reveal any juror bias. The court swears the chosen jurors to follow the law and gives other preliminary instructions, following which the lawyers give opening statements. The plaintiff then presents a case in chief in which the plaintiff's lawyer examines witnesses and offers exhibits, and the defense lawyer cross-examines the plaintiff's witnesses. When the plaintiff rests, the defense may move for a judgment as a matter of law. If the court denies the motion, then the defendant proceeds with the defendant's case in chief. When the defense rests, the plaintiff has the opportunity for rebuttal. Both sides give closing arguments. The court then instructs the jury with the law. The jury receives a verdict form and retires to deliberate. When the jury reaches a verdict, the foreperson reads the verdict in open court. The court or the parties' lawyers then prepare, and the court signs and files, a judgment consistent with the verdict. The losing side may file post-trial motions for new trial or judgment as a matter of law. Compelled enforcement of the judgment can add another layer of procedure if the losing party does not voluntarily comply.

Appeal. Jury trial limits the authority of judges to determining matters of law rather than fact. Where the right to a jury trial exists and at least one of the parties demands it, juries decide fact disputes, not judges. That practice means that appeals from jury decisions evaluate primarily legal rather than factual issues. Appellate courts respect the jury's role in evaluating the credibility of witnesses and the weight of the evidence. Review standards on appeal vary depending on the nature of the proceeding in the trial court. If the trial court dismissed the case without hearing evidence in a trial or other proceeding, then the appellate court gives no deference to the trial court's decision and instead simply reviews for legal error. If on the other hand the trial court heard evidence, then the appellate court will grant deference to the trial court's factual findings and reverse only for clear error.

Alternative Dispute Resolution. Alternative forms of dispute resolution, frequently referred to as ADR, begin with private negotiation, in which the lawyers help the parties share and evaluate information, generate options, adjust expectations, and communicate offers and counter-offers until the parties reach a voluntary settlement. Mediation is another form of ADR in which the lawyers and parties hire a private mediator trained in settlement techniques to meet with the parties to help them share and evaluate information, generate options, adjust expectations, and communicate offers and counter-offers until the parties reach a voluntary settlement. Another form is case evaluation, in which

112

the lawyers submit their clients' case to a panel of other lawyers who practice in the same field, and the panel places a settlement value on the case that the parties reject on penalty of paying the other side's attorney fees if they fail to improve their position through further litigation. Arbitration is another form in which the parties submit their dispute to a private arbitrator or panel of arbitrators, agreeing to be bound by the arbitration decision made after a streamlined process and hearing. Parties may use a combination of these means of alternative dispute resolution in any one case.

Criminal Justice. The criminal-justice system involves state or federal substantive law defining crimes, and federal and state constitutions providing procedural protections against over-zealous enforcement of those substantive laws. Most criminal prosecutions occur in the state courts under charges alleging state-law crimes. Yet federal criminal law enacted under Congress' commerce powers has an increasing reach, for example, through drug, firearm, and fraud laws. A single transaction or event may simultaneously implicate federal criminal law and the criminal law of one or more states. The double-jeopardy clause of the Constitution's Fifth Amendment prohibits multiple prosecutions on the same operative facts but does not prohibit both state and federal prosecution.

Constitutional Protections. Under the 14th Amendment, the Bill of Rights protects individuals against not merely federal but also state action. Constitutional protections make criminal procedure the focus of many criminal prosecutions. Criminal prosecutions are often not over whether the defendant committed the charged crime but instead whether the investigation and prosecution respect Fourth Amendment rights against unreasonable search and seizure, Fifth Amendment privileges against self-incrimination, and Sixth Amendment rights to confront adverse witnesses. Defendants invoke these rights through pretrial, trial, appellate, and post-conviction review proceedings. Courts decide criminal charges in an adversarial system pitting prosecution against defense. But criminal justice is also accusatorial, meaning that the prosecution must prove each element of the charge without the defendant's assistance. The prosecutor in a criminal case bears a much heavier beyond-a-reasonable-doubt proof burden than the preponderance-of-the-evidence proof burden in civil litigation.

Charging. When police investigation produces evidence of crime, public-employee prosecutors or district attorneys file charges with the court sometimes after obtaining indictments from grand juries. The court issues an arrest warrant, compelling the defendant to submit to police authorities or enabling authorities to apprehend the unwilling defendant. Within a one- to two-day period after arrest, the defendant appears before the court for arraignment on the charges, where the defendant admits or denies guilt, the court confirms or appoints counsel, and the court determines the terms of any bond if the defendant is to remain free pending trial. If the charges were without indictment, then the defendant has the right to a preliminary examination at which the prosecutor must show the court that there is evidence supporting the charges. If the prosecutor shows supporting evidence, then the court binds the defendant over for trial.

Pretrial and Trial. With the important exception of motions challenging the admissibility of evidence, pretrial motions and discovery are often less extensive in criminal cases than in civil cases. The opposing sides focus instead on preparing the case and defense, and on constitutional and statutory procedures such as speedy trial and confrontation of witnesses influencing strategy. The court may hold pretrial conferences to explore pleas. Trial then proceeds similarly to civil jury trials except that the lawyers in criminal cases may generally peremptorily remove potential jurors without limit. The prosecution and defense tend to question jurors more closely and remove more jurors than do the lawyers in civil cases.

Sentencing. The jury's verdict is not the end of a criminal proceeding but the beginning of sentencing and review phases. Sentencing usually takes place well after trial. Sentencing procedure often involves pre-sentencing investigation, sentencing report, challenges to sentencing report, victim-impact statement, and sentencing hearing. In death-penalty cases, the trial jury may reconvene to consider mitigating circumstances and decide or advise as to the ultimate penalty. A convicted and sentenced defendant may appeal conviction and sentence to an appellate court of the federal or state justice system that charged and convicted the defendant. Defendants convicted in state court may in habeas corpus proceedings request federal courts to review the constitutionality of their convictions, based on federal rights not adjudicated in the state proceeding.

Plea Bargaining. Although the criminal-justice system is adversarial and accusatorial, most criminal cases resolve without trial, either by dismissal of the charges or by guilty plea, in the latter case often after plea bargaining. Prosecutor and defense must inform the trial judge of a plea bargain. Trial judges are usually less involved in negotiations than they might be in civil litigation. Given the cost of punishment, complexity of rehabilitation, and collateral consequences of conviction, the public shows increasing interest in diversion programs, special criminal courts, and other emerging alternatives. Throughout criminal proceedings, prosecutors owe duties to the public and defendants such as to disclose exculpatory evidence. The adversarial nature of the proceeding makes critical the quality of representation in criminal defense. Juvenile-justice systems modify criminal law and procedure to emphasize supervision and rehabilitation while de-emphasizing retribution.

International Law. Until recently, law students could graduate without having given any significant thought to international law and still feel well qualified for the practice of law in most fields. Today though, globalizing economies, global migration, instant world communication, and increasing significance locally of world affairs combine to make international law increasingly important in domestic matters. International law has three sources: (1) treaties and conventions; (2) customary international law; and (3) general principles of law. The United States recognizes some United Nations conventions and has

115

entered into treaties. Customary international law involves rules and practices arising out of the conventions and treaties into which nations have entered. Customary international law may bind a nation and its citizens even when the nation has not entered into a treaty codifying the rule or practice. The third form of international law, general principles, restrict the domestic law of nations. Prohibitions against slavery are examples. These international laws engage American institutions, citizens, and their lawyers to ever-greater degrees. Yet globalization is a two-way street. Expect your law studies to reflect both the increasing influence of international law on domestic law and the increasing reach of American law internationally.

Comparative Law. Contrasting American law and procedure to the law and procedure of other systems helps you learn. For example, the U.S. adversarial system of justice contrasts with Continental inquisitorial systems where government officials, rather than private parties, pursue and prosecute causes. For another example, federalism in the United States differs from federalism in other countries, American states playing a significantly greater role in both public and private law than in other federal systems. American states also have significantly more comprehensive and influential court systems. America's strong federalism increases local involvement in government and citizen commitment to law. The common-law system of the United States, shared by England, India, Israel, most of Canada, Australia, New Zealand, South African, Ghana, and a few other countries, differs from Continental civil-code systems in other countries around the world. At the most general level, though, the greatest difference between the U.S. justice system and systems in other countries may be the substantial procedures and protections it affords.

Study. You represent an entrepreneur whom federal securities-fraud investigators have contacted regarding the entrepreneur's sales of shares in a foreign-based business to customers who lost their investments. Explain in writing to your entrepreneur client the civil- and criminal-justice systems through which others may hold the entrepreneur accountable for any law violations.

X. What Are a Lawyer's Roles?

Identity. Your ability to conceive of a healthy professional identity for lawyers can also build your commitment to preparing to join the profession. The legal profession has learned much about lawyer ethics in the decades since Watergate's wakeup call. Accreditation standards require law schools to provide ethics instruction. Yet ethics instruction is much broader than learning basic conduct rules to keep you from losing your law license in a grievance proceeding. Law school must help students develop strong, positive professional identity. Positive identity includes traditional roles and attributes like the lawyer as responsible advocate, public citizen, and member of a noble profession. Lawyers also advocate that clients, opposing parties, judges, witnesses, and others behave ethically. Strong, positive identity also includes maintaining balance and attending to wellness. Lawyers who live unhealthy professional and personal lives harm themselves and their law practices, partners, and services, and family members.

Professionalism. Lawyers must also demonstrate civility and professionalism. Lawyers develop a guiding sense of professional propriety that keeps their conduct and relationships civil even in, and especially in, vigorous disagreement with others. Lawyers know how to disagree without being disagreeable. Lawyers also participate in the profession. They attend bar association meetings, educate the public in responsible government, mentor youth and new lawyers, and promote diversity within the profession. Being a responsible, admirable, and effective lawyer has many satisfying dimensions. The following sections explore lawyer ethics and professionalism.

A. Conduct

Rules. Lawyers follow conduct rules that state bars and supreme courts adopt. Conduct rules govern the relationship between lawyer and client, activities of a lawyer as a counselor and advocate, organization and supervision of law practice within firms, and protection of the public. Lawyers find plenty of clear guidance on what to do and not to do. We all have intuitive understandings of ethics, but ethics training and guidance from clear conduct rules helps lawyers with special ethics issues that professional service raises. Lawyer conduct rules are both compulsory, meaning that lawyers must follow them, and aspirational, meaning that they encourage lawyers to engage voluntarily in better conduct. The following sections introduce several areas that lawyer conduct rules address.

Lawyer-Client Relationship. Conduct rules first address the lawyer-client relationship. Lawyers may generally represent whom they wish but must not represent clients in conflict with other clients. Lawyers and other members of their law firms cannot advocate on both sides of the same disputed matter. Lawyers must also generally accept court appointment to represent the indigent. Fees that lawyers charge clients must be reasonable in amount, even if clients have agreed to pay excessive fees. Lawyers must hold client funds separate from the lawyer's own funds. Lawyers must try to maintain normal relationship with clients who suffer from diminished capacity. Confidentiality rules prohibit lawyers from disclosing their clients' matters to others except under certain conditions.

Counselor and Advocate. Other conduct rules guide lawyers in counseling and advocating for their clients. Clients, not lawyers, determine goals for the representation including whether to settle civil claims or enter pleas to criminal charges. Lawyers may give clients legal, moral, ethical, social, economic, political, and other counsel on those matters. Lawyers must communicate truthfully, while advising clients independent of outside influences. Lawyers may discuss with clients the consequences of proposed courses of action including whether those actions comply with the law but must not counsel or participate in unlawful action. A lawyer may reveal a client's confidential information to prevent death or serious physical injury and to prevent substantial financial injury using the lawyer's services. Lawyers who represent organizations owe their duties to the organization, not its individual members. A lawyer who learns of an officer or employee's law violation must generally report that law violation to responsible superiors, including if necessary to the organization's board. Lawyers must not assert or maintain frivolous claims or defenses.

Law Practice. Conduct rules also govern law practice. State laws prohibit practicing law without a license. Practicing in multiple jurisdictions generally requires obtaining multiple licenses and uniformly requires complying with the conduct rules of each jurisdiction. Conduct rules also prohibit lawyers from assisting others in unauthorized practice. This prohibition means that lawyers must not allow secretaries, legal assistants, law clerks, investigators, and other unlicensed law firm staff to practice law. If lawyers engage with others in providing related professional services, such as financial services, then they must let clients know that lawyer conduct rules do not protect the clients as to those non-legal services. Lawyers must practice both diligently (no procrastinating) and competently (no substandard practice). Lawyers must also supervise subordinate lawyers and assistants so that those subordinates comply with conduct rules. Conduct rules prohibit false or misleading advertising, paying a non-lawyer for referring clients, and solicitation, meaning direct contact with potential clients whom the lawyer knows need legal services, for monetary gain.

Public Protection. Other conduct rules address how lawyers must act toward others who are not their clients. Lawyers must not make false statements of fact and must instead speak truthfully. They must not communicate with a third person about a legal matter when they know that another lawyer who has not approved the communication represents that person. Lawyer must also tell others with whom they communicate about a representation that the lawyer represents another person. They must also not give legal advice to others whose interest conflicts with the interest of the lawyer's client. Lawyers must tell the court about material adverse authority if the other side who should have cited the authority fails to do so and the court does not know of the authority. Lawyers must report other lawyers who violate conduct rules in ways that call into question their substantial fitness for law practice. When lawyers violate conduct rules, grievance boards may reprimand them or suspend or revoke their law licenses. Few lawyers suffer license sanctions despite rigorous rules, ample enforcement resources, and fair procedures. The vast majority of lawyers follow the conduct rules and are highly ethical.

Study. Your have learned through a nurse friend that a local lawyer has been visiting the hospital to solicit potential personal-injury clients and has also charged several of these clients excessive fees. You know that the lawyer's practices violate conduct rules. Explain in writing how you plan to address the lawyer's misconduct.

B. Duties

Standards. Lawyers do more than just comply with conduct rules. Lawyers also attend to basic duties guiding them in how to act in certain situations. The first of those duties is to meet the standard of care of competent attorneys. The common law of care (*tort law* as lawyers know it) imposes that duty. When a lawyer fails to act as a competent lawyer would act in a certain situation, and the lawyer's failure causes the client to lose something of value, then the lawyer has committed malpractice for which the lawyer or lawyer's malpractice insurer must compensate the client. The law imposes on lawyers the same duty of care that doctors, nurses, accountants, and other professionals owe those whom they serve. Most lawyers will never commit malpractice. They may make rare mistakes, but law practice may then provide opportunity to correct mistakes or otherwise avoid or minimize the harm that might flow from them.

Risk Management. Even as lawyers practice prudently to comply with the standard of care and avoid malpractice, they also manage malpractice and other risks. Clients have much at stake in their legal matters, including finances, property, income, employment, relationships, freedom, and even life. Lawyers manage the risks of law practice, both for themselves and their clients. Lawyers carefully document for clients the scope of responsibilities, keeping clear what they have agreed to do for clients. They follow procedures like calendaring, notice systems, file review, file sharing, conflict checking, associate supervision, performance reviews, and management meetings to ensure diligent and competent practice. Lawyers guard their expertise by taking continuing legal education, declining matters outside their practice area, and associating with experienced counsel to handle matters in new areas. Lawyers routinely maintain malpractice insurance to ensure that if any below-standard practice harms a client, then the insurance will compensate the client. State bars also maintain funds out of which to pay client losses due to attorney misconduct.

Legal Duties. Lawyers also comply with special statutes to protect the public against broader harm. Lawyers who collect debts comply with state and federal laws on debt-collection practices. Lawyers who represent publicly traded corporations comply with federal laws protecting shareholders from illegal activity by those who control the corporation. Lawyers and law firms comply with federal and state laws prohibiting discrimination by race, sex, age, religion, or disability, in public accommodations and services. Lawyers also comply with the laws governing others. Lawyers can lose their law licenses for civil or criminal fraud, theft, embezzlement, and other law violations that reflect dishonesty and untrustworthiness. They can also lose their law licenses for drunk driving, substance abuse, and financial irresponsibility, even while state bars have assistance programs to help lawyers overcome personal challenges that do not necessarily indicate unfitness for law practice.

Fiduciary Duties. Lawyers also have duties when entrusted with money, property, or interests belonging to others. Fiduciary duties differ from the above conduct rules and duties imposed by civil and criminal laws. Fiduciary duties arise out of the common law, probate codes and rules, and other statutory sources in specific areas. Lawyer trustees, conservators, guardians, executors, representatives, and administrators must show reasonable care and strict loyalty for the client, beneficiary, or ward whom they serve. Lawyers recognize and respect when fiduciary duties apply. Lawyers holding funds or property for clients must or serving as trustee or guardian ad litem must keep the interests of the client, trust beneficiary, or guardianship ward clearly in mind when dealing with banks, creditors, debtors, care providers, family members, and others. Lawyers recognize and respect their duty of trust and confidence, the breach of which requires them to make the client, ward, or beneficiary whole.

Study. You represent a client whom a careless driver seriously injured in a motor-vehicle accident, leaving the client unable to work. The client's prior lawyer neglected to file the client's case. Your research shows that the prior lawyer's delay now bars the case, which would have resulted in a substantial insurance recovery. Explain in writing to your client your plan to help the client with a financial recovery.

C. Qualities

Character. Lawyer ethics and professional identity involve more than conduct rules and duties. To stop at rules and duties would cheat the profession and public of what being a lawyer means. Lawyers benefit, and their clients and the public benefit,

124

when lawyers acquire, develop, and exhibit certain qualities. Think of those qualities as attributes, attitudes, and dispositions. No two lawyers are exactly alike. Yet lawyers develop and share attributes that make them better lawyers. Lawyers do not merely perform law services. As lawyers serve, they also become someone, exhibited by professional attributes. Similarly, lawyers carry and share professional attitudes, not merely that they react in certain ways but that they acquire a common outlook. They also exhibit shared dispositions, critical to the important role they play in the lives and futures of their individual and corporate clients. Explore below some of these attributes, attitudes, and dispositions.

Attributes. Lawyers are leaders. Whether the setting is a local public board or commission, the board of a charitable organization, or neighborhood gatherings over matters of common interest, people expect lawyers to think responsibly, communicate clearly, and act with vision, foresight, and discernment. Lawyers recognize perspectives and personalities, seeing significance in events, actions, and characteristics, where others see nothing. Lawyers stand courageously during their clients' crises, willing to risk and venture responsibly, calculating reasonably while ready to accept consequences. Lawyers have conviction, believing in pursuing good. Lawyers exhibit mastery, pursuing, acquiring, and conveying moral expertise. Lawyers act with composure. Lawyer are seldom ruffled, instead encouraging the trust and reliance of those whom they serve and even those whom they oppose and challenge. Lawyers exhibit stability, maintaining enduring characteristics while acquiring the trust of judges, commissions, communities, and clients. Lawyers are stewards, holding in trust the lives and fortunes of their clients and the welfare of communities.

Attitudes. Lawyers also hold certain attitudes, mental approaches, or stances that improve their professional acumen and services. Lawyers deliberate and reflect, especially on motives, consequences, and ethical dimensions of their actions and actions of others. They scrutinize and consider. Lawyers are

125

observers of people and their actions and reactions, constantly aware of the demeanor, mood, movement, and intention of others. Lawyers notice behaviors and patterns. Lawyers also serve and engage. They actively promote the well-being of others, employing their full capacities to engage not only clients but opposing parties, judge, profession, and public. Lawyers pursue excellence, expecting the best of themselves and others. Lawyers innovate, generating creative new solutions to old problems. Lawyers promote these attitudes among others through the desire to collaborate.

Dispositions. Lawyers also share dispositions that maintain and improve their performance, identity, and health as professionals. Lawyers prepare, constantly looking ahead, planning, and anticipating. Lawyers are lifelong learners and highly skilled in learning, growing professionally and personally throughout their careers. Lawyers are aware of their own thinking, preserving old and adopting new mental practices that improve their effectiveness. Lawyers self-assess their own competence against professional standards and the competence of one another, not in destructively competitive fashion but in fellowship as members of a profession. Lawyers integrate knowledge, skills, and ethics into judgment. They know how to combine and emphasize different dimensions for greatest effect in service of cause, client, and public. Lawyers are data-driven in their judgment, identifying, gathering, and examining measures on which to base their counsel. Lawyers understand decision-making, pursuing reliable processes when advising and deciding.

Study. You moved recently to a suburban city where you are one of only a few lawyers. The law partner who hired you into your small law firm has asked for your thoughts on developing your client base in this new locale. Explain in writing your plan to establish a network of local contacts from which you might find service opportunities.

D. Identity

Relationship. Ultimately, though, a lawyer's professional identity depends not on rules, duties, and qualities but on how the lawyer interacts with others. Identity arises through relationship. Lawyers follow rules, fulfill duties, and develop character to serve the needs of others through an integrated professional identity. Lawyers know and attend to who they are, in order that they may know and serve others. As lawyers develop their own positive professional identity, they become more aware of the identity of others. Lawyers have a fascination for and appreciation of people. They want to know what others like and dislike, how others' experiences differ from their own experiences, and what others need and value. Lawyers interact supportively with others, using inter-cultural skills to form effective service relationships with diverse individuals and populations. The emotional, interpersonal, social, and ethical adaptations of lawyers overcome insular culture. Consider three specific areas, (1) communication, (2) cognition, and (3) reference, in which lawyers adapt to provide effective law services to others.

Communication. Communication adaptations help lawyers transform their professional identity from constraint to asset. Lawyers know that people speak differently depending on their culture, education, emotional condition, and environment. Lawyers adapt their communication to fit client needs. Lawyers usually speak in consultative register, assuming that the hearer pursues advice in an exchange. Yet when stressed, vulnerable, and confused clients speak in dependent register, lawyers respond firmly and reassuringly until the client can move beyond dependency to reasoned thought. When a client speaks casually to test a lawyer's willingness to treat the client as equal, the lawyer matches the casual register to put the client at ease. When a client uses formal titles and last names, and refers to achievements and memberships, the lawyer recognizes that the client values role more than relationship or exchange. When a client makes cultural and scriptural references, the lawyer adjusts advice to the client's commitments and norms.

127

Cognition. Lawyers also modify their professional identity, advice, and service for clients' differing abilities. Lawyers identify client goals, recognize intermediate objectives that help clients reach those goals, and plan for accomplishing those objectives. They implement plans, assess plan progress, modify non-working plans, and identify when they have reached objectives and goals. Yet lawyers know that not all clients also do so. A client may begin a consultation without knowing what the client hopes to accomplish with the lawyer's service. The client may reasonably believe that identifying goals is fruitless. Lawyers recognize client limitations and adaptations, drawing on their own professional skills to help clients move forward with effective action. A client may be unaccustomed to planning, leading the lawyer to serve in ways that do not require client planning. Clients may not assess plan progress, instead taking the same ineffective action expecting different results. Lawyers help clients assess their actions when clients are unable to do so.

Worldview. Lawyers also recognize their own and their clients' reference systems, and modify their service accordingly. Clients base worldviews in family, social and ethnic history, popular or discrete culture, religion, educational and employment field, and personal experience and revelation. Lawyers know their own affinities and those of their clients. Lawyers value the family history, ethnicity, culture, faith, field, and personal experience of clients and others. Word choice, idioms, actions, dress, and demeanor provide lawyers with clues to adapt advice to draw on the strengths of, and also modify and overcome the limitations of, distinct reference systems. When clients reason in probabilities, lawyers advise as to probabilities while articulating limitations to probabilistic thinking. When clients reason in moral terms, lawyers help clients draw on those moral commitments. When clients reason pragmatically, lawyers emphasize the achievable. When clients reason emotionally, lawyers articulate emotional consequences to courses of action while proposing alternative viewpoints. Lawyers know the benefit and effect of reference systems, adapting advice accordingly to best serve clients, profession, and public. Lawyers can recognize and draw on multiple worldviews, to provide clients with greater insight and more-effective service.

Study. You represent an undocumented immigrant who through an interpreter indicates she wishes to file for asylum based on gang-related physical abuse and death threats for her refusal to smuggle drugs into the country. Your confused and fearful client is unsure whether to trust you, your office staff, or the law. Outline in writing for yourself and office staff how you will preserve and promote the client's trust as you complete your law services.

XI. What Do I Do with a Law Degree?

You have a wide array of choices over what to do with your law degree. For some students, that question becomes something of a problem. With so many choices, how do you decide what career to pursue? First, don't worry too much now about your future career choice. Law school will help you a great deal in narrowing your choices. Sound law schools offer many career-exploration activities like mentor programs, on-campus lunch-with-a-lawyer events, off-campus professional conferences, bar association and section memberships, internships, clinics, and more. Your professors and classmates will help you explore, as will your family and friends. Second, most of us have multiple careers. Your first job after earning your law degree will very likely not be your last. You may love your first job or you may not, but either way chances are good that your first job, while significant in itself, is also preparing you for your second job, and your second job for your third, and so on. Many stable and competent professionals have two, three, or four jobs in the first five to ten years of their career, simply because of new opportunities and professional growth. Yet thinking some now about how you will go about choosing your first job can help you get a head start in law school. When you have a goal or guide star, you tend to concentrate and energize, even if the goal or guide star changes over time. So consider the following framework for choosing a law or law-related career.

A. Know Yourself

Awareness. You have many things that you can do with a law degree, from practicing law to running a nonprofit, prosecuting or defending alleged wrongdoers, putting together complex business deals, negotiating a bond issue for a hospital or stadium, serving a government agency, or leading the nation as yet another lawyer president. Welcome those conversations when friends and family members ask what you plan to do with your law degree. Ask them what they think you'd be good doing. Learn about yourself through others. Come to know yourself. Professionals tend to have good introspection. Reflection on one's own performance, character, and preferences is a professional skill. Healthy self-examination is how lawyers improve their work and work-life balance. Develop greater awareness of your own unique character, affinities, personality, and interests, and greater capacity for making fruitful adjustments to reflect your attributes. Indeed, one fair response to the question of *why law* is that the degree program helps you learn about yourself. Tell that to others while also telling them the value of the rule of law as that least bit of social control that does the greatest good for the greatest number.

Affinities. One of the things that you might recognize about yourself is that your commitment to earning a law degree is a commitment to promoting peace, security, liberty, efficiency, economy, property, and other forms of human flourishing. To earn a law degree is to become effective at promoting that flourishing. As long as you have people seeking you out to help them, then you know that your work has value. Every client confirms implicitly that your work has meaning. That said, choose clients with whom you have an affinity, for whom you wish to work. Know the kinds of people whom, and plans and purposes that, you value and respect. Simply because the client values you doesn't mean that you will necessarily value the client. Some lawyers love helping government and corporate clients build roads and hospitals. Others prefer working for the individual client who uses those roads and hospitals for his or her own ends. Both works have value and meaning. One may be more for you than the other. Drawing on the commitments that you held before starting law school, including faith and philosophy, is perfectly appropriate and acceptable. Treat your law practice not just as a job or profession but also as a calling.

Models. To know the specific law work that is for you can be hard to decipher in advance. Studies of lawyers find that while new lawyers sometimes take the first year or two to find a conducive practice area, many senior lawyers deeply enjoy their work. Outsiders wouldn't necessarily know why that was the case, failing to see valuable things like the intellectual challenge of work, client relationships, work's ebb and flow, and work's important detail, artistry, subtlety, and craft. One way to choose a field is to choose a practitioner who enjoys it. Simply find a lawyer to respect, model, and emulate. Law school, through mentor, career, and networking programs, will help you do so. Consider the legacy that those lawyers are leaving, and think of the legacy that you, too, would like to leave. As you explore what commanding lawyers have accomplished, be prepared to exercise courage in making your own choice of pursuits. Face fears rather than run from them. Exercise the courage of your convictions.

B. Know Law Delivery

Service. In one sense, you need not be too concerned about choosing what you will do with your law degree because clients will tell you what to do. The privilege of law practice is the privilege of serving others. You need not have your own dream when your dream may simply be to promote the dreams of others. Finding happiness through its direct pursuit can be difficult, but you may find happiness and more in direct pursuit of a service career. Good lives and character, formed through diligent service, bring happiness in abundance. Your service, though, is a constrained service around which rules and respect for the rights and interests of others establish fair and reasonable bounds. Those necessary and helpful constraints mean that your skill, not your power, is what will advance your clients' dreams and interests. Indeed, one constraint is that although you can do many things with just a law degree, you need a law license to actually practice law. States or state bars license lawyers. If you know *where* you intend to practice but not *what* you intend to practice, then let the law fields in your state of practice help tell you what to practice. In other words, choose the field that will make you a living in the locale in which you wish to live. Don't decide to be a securities lawyer only to find out that you can't find such a job in the rural locale in which you need or prefer to live.

Income. You need not let the profession dictate how much you will work. Lawyers do work either full time or part time, whether those lawyers are in large or small firms, or certain law fields. Full-time work can be satisfying and enriching, but so can part-time work. Consider part-time law practice if you have other substantial obligations or want to pursue other interests that contribute to your professional development, and do not need full-time income. Indeed, let your financial plans help determine your career choice. Be frank about both your financial interests *and* your financial responsibilities. If you are not likely to be adept at generating new work, a skill that lawyers often call *rainmaking*, then you may need to join an established employer to do its work rather than have the pride and privilege of doing work that your skill and relationships originate. At the same time, let your goal to earn your own keep also guide you to build important knowledge, experience, skills, and relationships. You may not be a rainmaker in your first job but could be one in your second or third job depending on your experience. Be responsible not just to paying the bills today but also to being able to do better than pay the bills tomorrow. When choosing a law career or field, consider both your initial income needs and your future income goals. One career or field leads to another.

Choices. Your commitments and affinities, together with your service ethic and skill, will guide you into doing the right and best things with your law degree. Yet you still have the opportunity to choose law fields. Value and appreciate that you have choices. Have a plan even while you keep your options open. Think deeply and often about what you want to do and should do. For instance, you might think a little about which side you'd rather be on in your career. Many law fields have distinct sides, whether representing the government regulator or regulated interest, management or labor, prosecution or defense, developers or conservationists, employers or employees, husband-fathers or wife-mothers, or claimants or insurers. Would you like representing the educated or uneducated, rich or poor, or David or Goliath? Think, too, about the forum in which you would prefer to practice. Would you like to work in an office, agency, or courtroom setting? Would you like to travel locally for hearings and depositions or nationally and internationally for mergers and acquisitions?

Size. As already intimated, you have a choice as to for what size of an organization you would prefer to work. Nearly half of all lawyers in private practice work in solo practices or very small law firms. They do so largely because they like the responsibility, financial opportunity, and independence. Yet many lawyers instead work in firms of five to ten lawyers, ten to fifty lawyers, or fifty to one-hundred lawyers, or large national firms in the hundreds of lawyers or even international law firms up into the thousands of lawyers. Law firm size can have a lot to do with the culture, competitiveness, and formality of the workplace, the clientele, and the firm's expectations, resources, advancement opportunities, and employment policies, among other things. Your skill as a manager may have a lot to do with which size firm would be best for you. Larger employers usually have more management, expecting less management from a new employee such as you. A large firm may have well-developed support systems and well-trained support staff. If instead you are already a sound manager who likes to establish policy more so than follow it, and give direction more so than take it, then you might prefer a smaller firm or solo practice. Consider the size of your law employer as another way to begin to choose a career.

C. Know Law Fields

Practice Mix. So you have now seen that your practice field is not the only consideration or even necessarily the primary consideration in choosing what to do with your law degree. In fact, if you practice law, then you are likely to do so in more than one field. Law practice typically involves a mix of practice fields rather than just one field. Combining one practice field with another can be critical to your practice's success. Examples of closely related fields include worker's compensation and Social Security disability, intellectual property and licensing, employment rights and civil rights, estate planning and guardianship practice, or business advising and tax practice. If you practice in one of these fields, then you could readily practice in the other field because the skills and knowledge bases are similar, and clients may have needs in both fields. You may also choose to have a general practice rather than to specialize in one or more fields, letting your clients and their changing needs dictate your practice areas. Lawyers frequently learn new fields and may be competent in many fields. Specializing in one field or a few fields can raise your skill and reputation but is not always advisable or necessary. If you do decide to specialize, then you need not choose a traditional specialization field like the ones names just above. You may instead develop what lawyers call a *boutique* practice, one restricted to an unusual field such as Medicare planning, eminent-domain cases, or quit-tam (government-fraud) actions.

Practice Divisions. So when thinking about specializing, how do you organize the dozens or even hundreds of different law fields and boutique practices? One ready division is between litigation practice and transactional practice. Litigation, involving dispute resolution centered on courts or similar tribunals, requires strategic, advocacy, and negotiation skills, deployed in an adversarial setting. Some lawyers do nothing but litigation, while other lawyers do not litigate at all. Among litigators, sometimes also called *trial lawyers*, lawyers specialize in different litigation fields. The first big division of litigation fields is between civil litigation involving private actions between parties represented by private counsel, and criminal cases involving public charges by prosecutors against individuals (and also corporations) defended either by private practitioners or, in the case of the indigent defendant, public defenders. Some lawyers handle only civil cases, other lawyers handle only criminal cases, and some lawyers handle both. By contrast, transactional practice does not involve dispute resolution. Instead, transactional lawyers help clients put together deals, structure their relationships, order their affairs, and otherwise manage their business, family, and personal interests. Transactional lawyers may work closely at times with trial lawyers, referring cases to trial lawyers for resolution while accepting referrals of transactional matters from trial lawyers and consulting with trial lawyers over transactional issues. Law firms tend to have a mix of both transactional and trial lawyers.

Criminal Justice. Lawyers further specialize within the criminal-justice area. As just indicated above, the big division is between prosecutors whom the government employs on the one hand, and on the other hand lawyers defending those whom the government charges with crime. Lawyers do not prosecute and defend all at once. They instead practice only on one side at a time, although over the course of a career some lawyers do change sides. Yet on both sides, meaning prosecution and defense, lawyers may further specialize. Some prosecutors only pursue municipal ordinance violations for things like leaving one's grass unmown or one's disabled vehicle parked on the street. Other prosecutors will pursue misdemeanor charges, and others felony charges, while only a few may charge and try the most-serious cases for sexual assault, kidnap, or homicide. Some prosecutors may work in the child-support-enforcement division or in child abuse and neglect. On the defense side, some lawyers may handle primarily alcohol-related offenses like minor-in-possession, open-intoxicant, and drunk-driving charges. Other defense lawyers may handle only misdemeanors and minor felonies, declining more-serious felonies, particularly cases involving charges of violent crime. Some defense lawyers specialize in drug cases and

137

others in white-collar crime, such as securities or government fraud, and related license hearings. Some defenders will practice only in state court, while others may specialize in defending federal charges. Each criminal-justice field can have its own opportunities, challenges, and culture.

Civil Justice. Just like in the criminal-justice area, lawyers naturally divide civil litigation into many different fields. Some lawyers will handle virtually any kind of civil litigation. Most lawyers, though, will specialize in certain fields such as family law, involving paternity, child custody, and divorce, or juvenile law, involving abuse and neglect, guardianship, and delinquency, or perhaps bankruptcy law, collections work, and creditors' rights. Other trial lawyers handle primarily commercial litigation, helping to resolve disputes arising out contract breaches, violation of partnership agreements, and other broken business relationships, or probate practice, involving settling decedents' estates. Other trial lawyers handle primarily tort claims arising out of personal injury, wrongful death, or property damage, involving parties having no business relationship other than as to the liability insurance indemnifying the claims. Tort litigators are typically either plaintiff's lawyers representing the individual, including lawyers who specialize in sub-fields like medical malpractice, civil rights, or worker's compensation claims, or insurance-defense counsel whom the insurers retain to defend their insureds. Other trial lawyers handle employment disputes over discrimination and harassment, or wage-and-hours and labor-agreement disputes. Some trial lawyers will practice only in state court while others will concentrate their practices in federal civil litigation, where the parties may have national interests and the amounts in controversy may be greater. Some trial lawyers maintain boutique class-action practices representing large numbers of consumer claimants. While trial lawyers practice before judges and juries in trial courts, some litigators specialize in appellate advocacy, honing their research and briefs for close scrutiny by appellate judges and justices.

Transactional Practice. Transactional lawyers, like litigators, also specialize. One of the largest transactional fields has to do with estate planning, meaning drafting wills and trusts, and otherwise helping individuals and families plan to pass assets from generation to generation in an orderly manner. Estate planners further specialize in areas such as assisting family owners of businesses, planning large estates to reduce taxes, and Medicare planning for the long-term disabled. Other transactional lawyers are business planners, helping form, advise, and grow business organizations to maximize benefits for their owners and employees, and the communities in which the businesses operate. Consider business planning if your interest is in creating and sustaining valuable enterprises. Some transactional lawyers specialize in securities law for business organizations that plan to raise capital using public or private offerings of ownership interests. Other transactional lawyers practice intellectual-property law, dealing with copyright, trademarks, trade secrets, and other proprietary interests. Some transactional lawyers are tax lawyers, while others are real-property lawyers, structuring sound conveyances and ensuring good title. Some transactional lawyers specialize in insurance law, health law, or municipal law. Other transactional lawyers specialize in various areas of administrative law such as licensing, antitrust, immigration services, or environmental law. The options are many.

D. Know Law-Related Fields

In-House Counsel. While lawyers practicing in private for-profits firms deliver most of the nation's law services, many other lawyers pursue law careers as employees of agencies and entities, without private clients. In-house counsel is one such role in which your only client is your own employer, the corporation that employs you to advise and represent it in its legal matters. As in-house counsel, you may provide your employer with a wide range of legal services from addressing employment policies to reviewing service contracts and addressing risk management whether relating to regulatory and compliance issues or tort and contract liabilities. In-house lawyers benefit from the common interest and strong loyalties that they share with their employer who is simultaneously their only client. In-house lawyers also often supervise the work of outside lawyers whom the employer retains for litigation or other specialized law services. In-house lawyers may also provide their employer with a range of business, administrative, and leadership services that do not strictly involve law skills, including in some cases serving as the employer's chief executive.

Public Interest. Lawyers also serve in public-interest roles, devoted not to individual client service as much as to systemic change. Public-interest lawyers may work for a nonprofit employer representing pro bono clients who would otherwise have no representation. Public-interest lawyers step in where the private market for law services does not meet client and public needs. Lawyers form and operate nonprofit public-interest law firms and other organizations devoted to specific causes such as environmental litigation, wildlife-and-resource protection, fair-housing litigation, voting-rights litigation, government transparency and accountability, and other local, regional, national, and international causes. Lawyers work as employees of those firms and organizations, devoting their full time to advancing the public-interest cause. They also work for legal-services organizations providing direct representation to indigent clients in landlord-tenant, welfare-benefits, and family law matters. Public-interest firms and organizations may depend in part on public grants and private contributions but may also collect prevailing-party fees in successful cause litigation. While expecting public support, public-interest lawyers may also face public opposition given the sometimes-controversial and usually unsettled nature of their causes and so must maintain the courage and confidence of their convictions. Lawyers also serve in legislative and administrative careers as legislative counsel, legislative analysts, and representative staff. They also act in private for-profit and nonprofit employment, in lobbying and government-affairs positions.

Judicial Roles. Some lawyers of course become judges. Judging requires a special temperament. Judges do not choose their matters. Parties choose what judges decide, meaning that judges must often decide disputes that they would not have brought at all or brought in that fashion. The bane of judging is deciding disputes that the judge feels have no real place in court. Litigation can be a proxy for anything including mental illness, revenge or vendetta, and economic leverage or oppression. Judges face challenges even when the role is as simple as deciding clear and credible disputes. Law is vast and complex. Judges whose dockets are of general jurisdiction face formidable intellectual challenges knowing and applying as much law as they must. New judges with specialized dockets such as criminal law, family law, probate, and business court will soon develop specialized knowledge and expertise, yet even senior judges see new matters involving unfamiliar or changing law. Judging carries prestige, security (at least until the next election), fair compensation, and reasonable benefits, but its constraints are significant including some degree of isolation. Some lawyers start their careers as judicial law clerks, while other lawyers become career judicial-staff attorneys.

Military Lawyers. Many lawyers also serve as military lawyers. Military bases in their myriad functions must comply with law, rule, and regulation. Military servicemembers also need lawyers who are familiar with the peculiar terms, requirements, and benefits of military service, and who can counsel and represent them in both military matters and in civilian matters that military service affects. The military provides for these law services through the Judge Advocates General Corps also known as the JAG Corps. Each military branch commissions lawyer officers to serve in the Judge Advocates General Corps. To be a military lawyer in the Corps, you must join a service branch, whether Army, Navy, Air Force, Marines, as a candidate for the Corps. Once in the Corps, military lawyers perform a range of law services involving everything from international law, treaty, and convention, to rules of engagement, foreign law, court-martial

141

law and procedure, law, rule, and regulation having to do with the terms of military service, veterans-benefits law, federal and state criminal law for servicemembers performing domestic base operations, and civil law of all kinds from family law to estate planning, real-property law, and simple contract obligations. Military bases are like small cities with most of a city's many law issues. JAG Corps lawyers may find themselves assisting servicemembers with matters that lawyers in a civilian general practice also handle. JAG Corps service in effect combines two noble careers, military service and law, in one. These are just a few of the dozens of alternative careers that lawyers pursue outside of private practice.

Study. Even if you are completely unsure of your answer, decide now what you will tell the next person who asks you, "So, what kind of a lawyer are you going to be?" or "What law are you going to practice?" Begin to try out answers, listening carefully to how you sound to yourself and how the person you tell reacts to what you say. For more reflection on this important subject, read *Dear J.D.: What to Do with Your Law Degree.*

Conclusion

Law studies explore and expose fascinating and important social, moral, economic, and political conditions. Teaching law engages state and federal appellate and trial-court judges, managing partners from major law firms, trial lawyers who have won multi-million-dollar verdicts, prosecutors, public defenders, United States attorneys, and corporate counsel for major multi-national corporations. In law school, the most committed and insightful lawyers guide, coach, mentor, support, encourage, and challenge the most inquisitive learners, to acquire knowledge, skills, and identity on which the world's shape, survival, and prosperity depend. This introduction should help you appreciate, enjoy, and benefit from the rich opportunities that law school affords. Let law's practice draw you, as law has drawn the courageous, committed, and effective before you. If you approach law studies properly and prepare earnestly for law practice, then you will receive your just reward in a satisfying, fulfilling, and meaningful service career. Law school holds the promise of being a transformative experience. Ultimately, personal transformation occurs when you connect your life with greater things, which in the case of law is to create and preserve the conditions for a just, free, and flourishing society. You could choose very few greater pursuits to which to devote your education.

Acknowledgments

The author acknowledges the support of the author's employer Western Michigan University Cooley Law School and its President and Dean Don LeDuc. The author further acknowledges the support of the law school's leadership team, particularly Associate Deans Christine Church, Paul Zelenski, and Laura LeDuc, with whom the author works on curriculum, student services, and assessment. The author also acknowledges the contributions of colleagues on the law school's faculty, particularly David Tarrien, Tonya Krause-Phelan, Victoria Vuletich, and Devin Schindler with whom the author shares an instructional-design project. The author also acknowledges the expert contributions of Western Michigan University instructional-design research lab Director Dr. Doug Johnson who (with the author) co-authored the book *Preparing for the Bar Exam*, from which the author drew portions of this book. The author also drew portions of this book from his prior book *Dear J.D.: What to Do with Your Law Degree*. The author also acknowledges the editorial insights of lawyer John Mashni and especially law student Kris Johnson without which the book would not have taken useful shape.

About the Author

Nelson Miller is a professor and associate dean at Western Michigan University Cooley Law School who practiced civil litigation for sixteen years before teaching law for the past thirteen years. He has conducted complex civil litigation in business, civil-rights, products-liability, plane-crash, helicopter-crash, medical-malpractice, and other cases in the state and federal trial and appellate courts. Dean Miller has also published over 30 books and dozens of book chapters and articles on law, law practice, and personal and professional development including *The Law Student's Guide, The Law Graduate's Guide, Injured – Seriously!, Dear J.D.: What to Do with Your Law Degree, Lawyer Finances,* and *Top 100 Questions Friends & Family Ask a Lawyer.* The State Bar of Michigan recognized Dean Miller with the John W. Cummiskey Award for pro-bono service, Western Michigan University Cooley Law School gave him its Great Deeds Award, and the Harvard University Press book *What the Best Law Teachers Do* included him in its study.

Other Law Books by Nelson Miller

A Law Student's Guide

A Law Graduate's Guide

Dear J.D.: What to Do with Your Law Degree

Preparing for the Bar Exam

Lawyer Finances

Entrepreneurial Practice

Cross-Cultural Law Service

Injured — Seriously!

The Top 100 Questions Friends & Family Ask a Lawyer

How to Get a J-O-B

The Faithful Lawyer

CPSIA information can be obtained
at www.ICGtesting.com
Printed in the USA
FFOW03n1203011116
28949FF